D1664298

Magic @ Work
by Christian Vandsø Andersen
www.vandsoe.dk
Published by Plazeebo Publishing

Illustrated by Majbrit Vandsø Andersen
Layout by P Haagen · pingvin.biz

ISBN: 978-87-974121-3-8
1st edition 2023
Printed by KDP

SET LIST

Please Allow Me To Introduce Myself 6

Welcome to the jungle 13

Whole Lotta possibilities 19

Penny Lane 29

School's Out 41

Interlude 53

Bohemian Rhapsody 61

All Along the Watchtower 79

Break on through (to the other side) 89

Come Together 97

(I can't get no) Satisfaction 105

Stairway to Heaven 113

Nothing Compares 2 U 119

Who are you 127

Another brick in the wall 139

You can't always get what you want 151

A momentary lapse of reason 161

Speaking Words of Wisdom 173

I Want To Break Free 191

Words Don't Come Easy 201

The Ace of Spades 213

I Feel Good 223

Space Oddity 243

Encore 253

Coda 𝄋 259

WARNING: MAY CONTAIN TRACES OF SUPERPOWERS.
PROCEED WITH CAUTION.

FOREWORD

"Children are our role models". Three years after joining the LEGO® Brand Group, following a long career in management consulting, I am still learning the power of the core belief of LEGO. When every day is "bring your inner child to work day", the environment fosters the creativity, fun and learning that we all experience in the LEGO Brand. Yet even this organisation has its outliers – colleagues who don't so much think outside the box but rather help us see a world without boxes. Christian is one of them.

Christian and I first met when he was giving a training course to a broad group of senior executives. Ostensibly the topic was 'Agile' but the audience that day was treated to a magical mystery tour, learning about complexity, coaching, storytelling and of course mentalism.

Since then Christian and I have had many opportunities to work together and have even caught a few magic rabbits (you'll shortly be learning about them). Yet I can never predict what Christian will contribute to a discussion, which always makes for an exciting meeting.

This book distills Christian's polymath wisdom into a rich yet digestible read. He draws on his experience in science, philosophy and coaching, adds a pinch of empirical learnings from his career at the LEGO Group and mixes it all into a magical story with captivating insights and tangible examples.

We all need a bit more magic in our lives, and I hope you get as much from reading this book as I did. You might even catch a magic rabbit or two.

PAUL WILLMOTT
DIGITAL ADVISER AT KIRKBI AND FOUNDER OF MCKINSEY DIGITAL

PLEASE ALLOW ME
TO INTRODUCE MYSELF
I'm a man of wealth and taste

The nature of my game might be a bit puzzling, so I reckon a short introduction might be in order.

I hold a Major in Computer Science with a minor in Mathematics from Aarhus University and a Master's degree from the Institute of Learning and Philosophy from Aalborg University. I have studied leadership at IMD – International Institute for Management Development – a private business school in Lausanne, Switzerland.

This background has led me to hold senior leadership positions at various companies. At the time of writing, **I am Vice President at the LEGO Group** working out of the headquarters in Denmark, creating digital experiences to delight our consumers.

I AM ALSO A MAGICIAN AND A MENTALIST CREATING EXCITING AND CAPTIVATING EXPERIENCES FOR AUDIENCES WORLDWIDE.

In various lore and mythologies, the magician usually plays the role of wisdom and transformation. The magician in Tarot Cards is the character that moves things from imagination to reality through sagacity and knowledge. The mythical description of the magician is not lost on me – I am fully aware of all the stories and mythologies.

However, the magic we discuss in this book is not that kind. We are talking instead about magic used for entertainment using sleight of hand or verbal acuity. This kind of magic has led me to drive massive transformations and has been my companion in a stellar career. While it might have been easier to write a philosophical book about mythology, this is a practical book about methodology.

I feel privileged to have had an extraordinary career as both a senior executive and a magician. My purpose with this book is to enable you to learn or, at the very least, be inspired to improve your business, career, or yourself – perhaps even all of them.

Neither the leadership path nor the magic path was something I had planned. It was an unexpected journey.

Becoming a leader is an emerging part of my career rather than a goal. Even though the people part became my primary passion for me, it is not just about leading my team. It is also about leading stakeholders, customers, and circumstances. Over the course of this unexpected journey, I have discovered that I have a knack for multifaceted leadership. It's something I find deeply fulfilling and the way I can bring the most value.

WHEN I WAS ON STAGE AS A MAGICIAN, I NEVER TOLD ANYONE THAT I ALSO HAD A DAY JOB AS A SENIOR EXECUTIVE.

AND AT MY DAY JOB, I RARELY TOLD ANYONE THAT I WAS A MAGICIAN AT NIGHT.

HOWEVER, MY MAGIC IS HIGHLY INFLUENCED BY MY LEADERSHIP.

AND MY LEADERSHIP IS HIGHLY INFLUENCED BY MY MAGIC.

I started my magic career doing **Close-up magic.** As the name implies, this is magic best enjoyed up close and personal. As opposed to traditional stage magic, where the wires and trap doors might be visible if you come too close, this type of magic encourages the spectator to pay close attention. Traditionally, close-up magic is performed with cards and coins, but anything small enough to be carried will work. I fell in love with card magic and the magic of cards. Every time you shuffle a deck of cards, you create something the world has never seen before. That in and of itself is magical. The possible permutations of 52 cards are 52! (the exclamation mark is read "factorial," meaning that you multiply every number from 52 to one, so 52 x 51 x 50 x 49...). That number is so large that it exceeds the number of atoms on earth.

Card magic is often done using **sleight of hand**. That is, you alter the position of one or more cards unseen to the spectator. This might seem counter-intuitive to the close-up idea because surely it is more difficult to manipulate a deck of cards right in front of a spectator who is encouraged to look closely. As it turns out, the more closely someone pays attention, the easier it is to "cheat," using another methodology of magic called misdirection. Misdirection is a powerful tool in magic, and we will explore this further in the section about curiosity.

Later in life, I became interested in mentalism.

A MENTALIST IS SOMEONE WHO READS MINDS AND INFLUENCES PEOPLE THROUGH HYPNOTIC SPEECH PATTERNS AND SLEIGHT OF MOUTH.

A mentalist pretends to have the power of mind control through increased mental capabilities and heightened sensory acuity. A mentalist usually uses archaic words and academic discourse, so it is the perfect role for me to play. I fully admit I am a bit eccentric and somewhat of a literary nerd. My scientific background influenced my way of speaking, and the role of a mentalist isn't that far from my personality.

The mechanisms a mentalist claims to use are not grasped out of thin air. You can hypnotize people during a normal conversation – it's a field called conversational hypnosis or sometimes covert hypnosis[1]. You can, to an extent, control people's minds by controlling their choices. You can read people's minds and tell if they are telling the truth or lying. Having spent many years pretending to read and control minds on stage, I discovered the real secrets behind these skills.

Now then, this might sound like a chicken and egg statement. How can I be on stage doing mind control and only later learn the secrets behind it? Well, as with many of the points in this book, there are several layers to this.

First, I realized that there is such a thing as mind-control. Then, on stage, I pretended to be able to control someone's actions and thoughts using methods from the magician's toolbox. To make the narrative more captivating, I researched everything I could on the subject and used words from that research. And every so often, this research leads to an unexpected result – I learned how to do it for real.

Mind control is not just something we see on TV. You can plant false memories in people's minds[2]. It's called confabulation[3], and it's not only the name of the psychological term but also the name of several magic effects simulating it. We prefer to call them "effects" rather than tricks, as it is more about the impact than the trick itself.

The scientist in me pursued the psychological, biological, or physical theories behind them, and distilled what methodologies could be used outside the realm of entertainment.

We will explore the following areas through the lens of magic and mentalism.

INNOVATION
LEADERSHIP
LEARNING
INSPIRATION
INFLUENCING

During the exploration, we will become acquainted with complexity theory, sensemaking, and the rhetorical secrets of charismatic speaking. We will also dive into some of magic's "real" secrets. While some may be excited to learn the real secrets of magic, others might be concerned that this is a burden of knowledge. According to a study from 2017, carrying secrets can indeed be harmful[4], but that only goes for secrets that would be harmful to you, should they be publicly known. So, you can proceed with your mind at ease – the secrets you will learn will enlighten and delight you.

If you are of the younger generation, reading an entire book can be a challenge, as you are probably used to the short-form content from social media. I applaud you for reading the book despite that and to reward you, here's a cheat list of the most essential chapters.

If you read nothing else, I urge you to dive into:

"SCHOOL'S OUT" – a novel approach to the learning organization

"BOHEMIAN RHAPSODY" – my take on leadership in complexity

"BREAK ON THROUGH (TO THE OTHER SIDE)" – how to boost innovation and motivation with a single concept

"NOTHING COMPARES 2 U" – you are not really you in an organization. But then, who are you?

If you have the stamina to read the full book, let's spend a few pages getting to know what you are about to learn.

WELCOME TO THE JUNGLE

A few things to be aware of as we enter the world of

MAGIC, LEADERSHIP, AND POLYMATHY

Sharing "secrets" seen as sacred by the community that created them can be fraught with perils. Bruce Lee's teaching of Kung Fu to people of the Western world was controversial because traditional Kung Fu practitioners believed that the art should only be passed down within Chinese culture and to Chinese individuals. They felt that Lee was diluting the authenticity and purity of Kung Fu. It resulted in the famous fight between Bruce Lee and Wong Jack-man in 1964. Wong felt Bruce Lee was undermining the traditional Chinese martial arts by teaching it to Westerners who could never fully understand or appreciate the cultural and philosophical aspects of Kung Fu. He challenged Bruce Lee to a fight to get him to stop teaching outsiders. Wong Jack-man was a popular and well-respected martial artist of his time and wanted the fight to be public. However, when the fight eventually did happen, it was behind closed doors, so we will never know who won.

I hope my teaching of magic principles will be less controversial. Persistent readers will be rewarded with more treats as the journey progresses. And who knows, you might become your generation's Bruce Lee, revolutionizing your industry and introducing new and exciting techniques to the masses.

THE BOOK WILL INTRODUCE NEOTERIC PRINCIPLES AND NOVEL CONCEPTS THAT HAVE EVOLVED OVER MANY YEARS THROUGH THE COMBINATION OF MAGIC, BUSINESS, AND SCIENCE.

My original research is published in my master theses, but none of my university masters included the magical aspect, which is published here for the first time. You, dear reader, possess imagination, wisdom, and perseverance – qualities that will serve you well in unlocking the mysteries these pages now unfold. While some concepts may initially seem obscure or implausible, your inquisitive mind and thirst for discovery will guide you.

Bundled with the concepts of magic, it will give you practical tools and methods to grow your business, your team, or yourself. The magician reading this book will learn about leadership, and the leader reading this book will learn about magic – including tricks you can perform the next time you are giving a presentation. My hope is that you will emerge informed, delighted, and, hopefully, with insight you didn't have before.

You will notice a small superscript number at the end of some statements[5]. This is a reference to a book, journal, or scientific article, which you can find in the endnotes at the end of the book. References substantiate claims to encourage thoughtful engagement rather than blind acceptance. The citations are not there just to add credibility and breadth to the research; they are also meant as helpful resources to dive into if you find a particular topic especially interesting.

As an added benefit, this also qualifies the book to be used as part of a teaching curriculum.

As with everything in life, treat information with critical thinking. There is no "magic" of the supernatural kind in this book. Even when discussing stopping time or becoming invisible, you will find the appropriate scientific references and explanations. Note that just because a reference substantiates a claim it does not make it true; it just adds credibility. If you read elsewhere that "studies show" without a citation, you cannot take whatever comes next seriously. If there are citations, chances are the claim is more credible. Either way, knowledge of the nature of science helps us understand and accept some of the exciting things we will explore[6].

BEFORE WE START, I WANT TO EXTEND MY GRATITUDE TO MY WORKPLACE – THE LEGO GROUP.

The LEGO Group is a place where creativity is everywhere – not just in the products but also in leadership. Working in a creative and innovative environment has been an advantage because my approach to leadership was appreciated. I knew when I joined the LEGO group 15 years ago that this was the place I wanted to work for the rest of my life.

It is important for me to say that the concepts and ideas presented in this book are not connected to, nor endorsed by, the LEGO Group. The journey we will embark on is solely my own, but I still believe I owe a lot to my workplace for being inclusive and allowing this unexpected leadership journey. So, thank you to the LEGO Group for being an awesome leadership playground. And a big thank you goes especially to all my colleagues and friends with whom I have worked for so many years.

Now, let's open up the floor by discovering the powers of the imaginary. We will explore how to move a problem into the imaginary world and back into reality once we have found solutions we would never have thought of otherwise.

WHOLE LOTTA POSSI-BILITIES

Thinking outside the box of reality to

INCREASE
INNOVATION

Most people remember when the internet suddenly buzzed with strange images of cats in space and large portions of text seemingly created by deceased philosophers. When AIs became publicly available, they started a revolution. Evidently, these AIs gained immediate traction, and soon the number of images and text posted on the internet generated by AI surpassed content generated by humans.

AIs can do this because a vast amount of data has trained the models. Most of our "high quality" data, such as encyclopedias and books, have been digitized, and paintings have been photographed, so there is more than enough data available to have an AI create images in the style of Vincent van Gogh or Pablo Picasso.

But here's the thing. While a generation in human terms is measured in decades, an AI generation is measured in nanoseconds. They are quickly consuming the world's information – at least human creations. Scientists predict that we are quickly running out of data[7], and soon the AIs will be trained by data generated by AIs. This could lead to "inbreeding", as too few new genes are added to the gene pool. The results from the various AI tools will essentially be echo chambers repeating variations of existing knowledge.

I see this as a huge problem because the diversity and variations of shareable information will suffer. I predict that human creativity will see a renaissance, and I humbly propose the following process for innovation for humans, by humans. Well this– and a bit of magic. There are a lot of myths about human creativity, and especially the types of people that can become creative geniuses. The good news is that they are just that. Myths. Everyone can be creative[8].

We need creativity, discovery, and new ideas. While AIs can answer almost any question we might throw at them, they cannot produce new knowledge. AIs will not discover X-rays or penicillin. They will not fight for equal rights or find a historical artifact that changes history by excavating archeological sites. While AIs can create music, images, or text that seems original, it is still trained by and based on human-created data. The originality might be due to patterns or combinations we haven't considered, but true originality will come from you.

I am often described as an optimist because I can see possibilities and options in challenging situations and am persistent in finding solutions. Someone once called me pollyannaish. At first, I thought the word was idioglottic, and I learned that this wasn't a compliment, as it means someone who is overly optimistic even when there aren't any solutions to whatever problem we face. I've also been called an erudite and a lexophile, referring to my appreciation for language and the use of words in expressive ways. This book is generally designed to be easy to read, and the occasional use of archaic words is deliberate. It is the thing that goes bump in the night, waking the reader, bringing them back to reality.

My optimism could be an artifact of my belief that everything is possible. Or rather, something being "impossible" is not a reason to stop.

Magic and innovation may seem like unlikely bedfellows, but when we take a closer look, the two are more closely intertwined than we might think.

AT THE HEART OF MAGIC AND INNOVATION IS THE ABILITY TO SEE BEYOND WHAT IS CURRENTLY POSSIBLE, IMAGINE A DIFFERENT REALITY, AND CREATE SOMETHING ENTIRELY NEW.

As a lifelong student of magic, I have found that the principles of magic can be applied to any field, including business and innovation. By embracing the magical mindset, we can break free from conventional thinking and tap into our imaginations to create genuinely groundbreaking solutions. In this chapter, we will explore how the principles of magic can be used to drive innovation, drawing on my experiences as a magician and leader in an innovative company. We will explore practical tips and techniques for harnessing the power of imagination, breaking through creative barriers, and turning seemingly impossible ideas into reality. Magicians do not see the impossible as equivalent to the unachievable. Impossible simply implies that something is not feasible in its current state or with the current capabilities.

This belief has helped me constantly push boundaries and find new solutions as a leader.

I have found that this approach – the magical approach – is a powerful metaphor for innovation. Depending on the industry, enabling innovation is a core part of leadership. I have participated in more innovation workshops than I can count, and the number one limiting factor has always been "reality". As the ideas flow, they are quickly killed with the (not unfair) argument that it is impossible. However, as we shall explore, not all ideas deserve to be killed off this early.

POSSIBLE MEANS "POSSESS THE ABILITY".
THAT IS, "POSSIBILITY" IS TIGHTLY LINKED TO
"CAPABILITY", AND CAPABILITIES CAN BE BUILT.

IMPOSSIBLE IS, THEREFORE, A PASSING STATE
WHICH CAN CHANGE WITH TIME.
IF SOMETHING IS TEMPORARY, IT SHOULD NOT
BE A PERMANENT LIMITATION.

This is an opportunity to create the space for more serendipitous processes, where unexpected discoveries and unplanned ideas emerge, proven to increase rapid innovation[9].

When I started to create magic effects, it was natural to follow the procedure of "effect first, a method later". After all, that was what my mentors told me. I may not have understood this profoundness initially, but that might have been to my advantage. As I created more and more effects and became somewhat successful as a part-time magician, I deeply valued this way of working. It is incredibly liberating, and the feeling you get when bringing the effect into reality is as thrilling as watching it unfold as a spectator.

We will use the word "real" to describe things that would be real to you and me. Reality as we know it. We will use the word "imaginary" to describe something that we know is not real. We know that James Bond is not real – even if we can clearly see him on the screen, we know it is an actor imagining what it is to be James Bond, but we enjoy believing in the illusion.

As a leader, you may develop people, processes, or products. The approach I describe is invariant to what you produce and, therefore, not

limited to innovation. It's all about staying in the imaginary space as long as opportunities are generated.

I notice that constraints come and go. If I had allowed them to constrain me, the process would end once the conditions were violated. For a while, you might want to break the laws of physics. Still, as the process continues and you get more clarity on what you want, you might achieve the outcome without breaking fundamental laws of physics because those specific parts of the idea-space have turned into something else. It is like in math when you work with variables in an equation that might look impossible to solve. But then, after working on the equation, some of the variables cancel each other out or disappear in different natural ways. This is like a typical creative process where the beautiful vase would never have been real without the excess clay left on the apron.

THE PRINCIPLE OF ADDING SOMETHING THAT WILL DISAPPEAR AGAIN IS SOMETIMES REFERRED TO AS THE CAMEL PRINCIPLE, NAMED AFTER AN OLD PUZZLE:

"An old man passed away, leaving ½ of his camels to his oldest son, 1/3rd of his camels to the middle son, and 1/9th to the youngest son. Upon opening the stables, they found that he had left them 17 camels. But you can't split 17 into ½, 1/3rd, or 1/9th without cutting some camels in half. They turned to their wise neighbor for help. 'Here, take my camel', the neighbor answered. They now had 18 camels, and the oldest got 9 (that's half of 18), the second got 6 (that's a third), and the youngest got 2 (that's a ninth). That leaves one camel, which the wise neighbor got back, and everybody was happy."

Adding and then taking back a camel helped solve an otherwise impossible problem.

As long as the solution space increases, it is okay to add complexity. The process will remove that complexity once we have the right solution. The camel puzzle is an example of a problem that cannot be solved. But, by adding a camel only to take it back again, the problem is suddenly solvable.

I remember being invited into the "inner circle of magicians" and joining a workshop, creating new effects—the almost euphoric feeling of being omnipotent set the scene for some marvelous ideas. As I was listening to the experienced magicians discuss new developments, I was first confused before being flabbergasted. They talked about ideas and effects that I, a man of science, knew for a fact would be impossible to achieve. After a while, I immersed myself in the universe of imagination, and we talked about all the wonderful effects we wanted to create until late that night.

Later, when I saw my newfound colleagues perform, I would recognize the impossible effects we were imagining, brought to life in a real magic show.

There is a bit of a mental hurdle to get over when learning magic, and I reckon it is a similar hurdle when we try to use the trade of the magicians in leadership. The hurdle, specifically, is that you begin in the imaginary world where there are no constraints. My own experience is that people tend to bring at least some constraints from reality to imagination. Core rules of the universe. The laws of physics. But then again – what are the laws of physics, and do they even exist? I could argue that what we call laws of physics are just mathematical models that seem to model reality. And when I say "seem", it is because we are constantly finding situations where these laws do not apply. We all learned Newton's laws of physics in school, only to be told when we went to university that Einstein proved them wrong.

We are probably too concerned about being correct these days. While Newton's laws might not, strictly speaking, be accurate, they are instrumental in many areas of mechanical physics. Even completely wrong theories can produce something good. In the olden days, we believed that combustible materials contained "phlogiston". It was a fire-like element that was released during combustion. As scientists did experiments to validate this hypothesis – that combustible elements contained phlogiston – they discovered another element that opened many other doors. They discovered oxygen, which is a necessary element of combustion, while at the same time discarding the idea of phlogiston.

LET'S CONTINUE DESCRIBING THE MAGICAL PROCESS.

To use the magical process, we must accept that everything is possible. Whatever impossibilities we will encounter will disappear in the final solution. Sometimes the impossibilities will disappear by themselves, and sometimes we will resort to a process called the illusion phase.

Impossible ideas are just as good as possible ones so long as you have a methodology to make the impossible possible.

In magic, as in product development, you never know if a trick is good until you have tested it on a real audience. To begin the validation, you hypothesize that your creation will achieve a given result. When you have successfully created a hypothesis, it needs to be tested. To do that, we need to transform it. Fortunately, most of our audience (customers or spectators) live in the real world, not the imaginary one.

Some ideas will have changed so much while expanding the solution space that they are immediately ready to transform into reality.

Some of the ideas will need to go through a process that's standard in magic but will be novel to the concept of leadership. It is the illusion phase, which we will explore in the next chapter.

PENNY LANE

SO WHAT DO WE DO WHEN WE HAVE A GREAT IDEA IN THE IMAGINARY SPACE AND WANT TO IMAGINE IT BEING REAL?

We create the illusion of it being real through a series of questions. When we look into the imaginary world from the real world, we do so through a lens called "illusion," where we get to play with the imagination. Literally.

THE WORD "ILLUSION" STEMS FROM THE LATIN "ILLUDERE" WHICH TRANSLATES TO "TO PLAY WITH."

The illusion phase is a transcendence of imagination into reality.

WHEN WE WATCH A MAGIC EFFECT, WE ARE LOOKING FROM REALITY INTO THE IMAGINATION THROUGH THE LENS OF ILLUSION.

"As I lift the coin in my hand, gently rubbing it, it will disappear into thin air as I blow on my fingers."

That could be part of the hypothesis, but there are vestiges of the impossible in the sentence. Physical objects cannot vanish into thin air.

We are going to ask an illusion question:

"What would it look like if it were possible?"

Sometimes, we are exposed to new or inexperienced magicians in the media. I recently saw a magician in a talent show on TV claiming he could make a coin vanish. He picked up the coin and wrapped it in a red silk scarf. When he removed the silk, the coin had vanished. The judges rightfully critiqued the act with, *"If you really could make a coin disappear, why wrap it in a red silk scarf?"*. The magician forgot to ask himself the illusion question.

"What would it look like if it were possible?"

The magician might hypothesize: *"When I scoop the coin off the table into my hand, I will secretly let the coin drop into my lap. I will still hold my hand with the appearance of an object, and if I gently rub my fingers on the non-existent coin, it will reinforce the idea that it is still there. After all, who rubs nothing? I will look directly at my hand, slightly gesturing and moving it upwards, as I talk about the coin. I will coordinate my words, my gaze, and my hand movements. The audience will believe I still have the coin in my hand, making it seem impossible when I show that it has vanished."*

The illusion question is a hypothesis within the hypothesis that needs to be tested with a real audience. Will the audience buy the subterfuge just described and think the coin is still in the hand, or will they wonder why a coin was suddenly in the magician's lap?

Magicians do a lot of audience testing, and hypotheses in the business world are no different. Will the spectators buy into the illusion, or will they shake their heads in disbelief? The only way to know is to test it.

Illusion questions are not just for developing effects or products. Let's look at an example where you are developing people. This will demonstrate how to solve the issue in the imaginary world and then use the illusion questions to move the solution into reality.

You are coaching Kim, a new leader with a problem on the team.

Kim explains: *"It's Joshua. He has been here forever and is the only person who knows the ins and outs of the system. He is fully aware of that, and it creates toxic behavior. He constantly threatens to leave, knowing very well that his knowledge is essential, so I let him get away with this behavior, although it hurts the team."*

The issue is relatively easily to resolve in the imaginary world, but in reality, Kim feels it is impossible.

Enter an illusion question.

"What would it look like if it were possible?"

You are not asking Kim for a tangible solution.

You are asking how a solution would appear if it were possible.

It is a hypothesis within the hypothesis, and the "appear" gets help from the imaginary world because of the illusion.

The illusion question frees Kim to think without restrictions and enables conversation and ideas.

Kim answers: *"The team would work with a learning mindset, gaining enough knowledge to understand, operate and continuously develop the system."*

That might be the beginning of the hypothesis Kim is forming. The liberating structure of the illusion question helps with phrasing an idea regardless of constraints, as it is just an illusion.

Kim notices that the answer to the illusion question does not involve Joshua.

To get the team to have a "learning mindset" and make it clear that they are now responsible as a team, Kim concludes: *"I will move Joshua to another team. He will be nearby and available for questions if the team is stuck. They might ask him 100 questions on day one, but it will probably be 90 on day two and so forth. Joshua might decide to leave, but this way, the team has been focused on knowledge transfer because they know how it feels not having his expertise directly on the team."*

The key point is that instead of asking, *"How can this be possible?"* ask, *"How would it look if it was possible?"*

This momentarily lifts the cognitive load of reality and lets the person play with the imagination.

It is much easier to describe how it would look if it were possible than to explain how it could be possible.

Still, the transcendence into reality has already begun by processing the illusion.

The key point is the space you create for the person you coach.

THE COGNITIVE LOAD OF REALITY IS MUCH LARGER THAN WE THINK.

The burden of reality is lifted by moving the subject into the imaginary world, and solutions become much more accessible. Once a solution is found, we use the illusion questions to make it real.

You may choose different types of illusion questions as long as they help move the process forward. Anything you can imagine being true can act as a starting point. The example with Kim is reminiscent of the Miracle Question[10] used in therapy, and many great examples of illusion questions are found in systemic practices. The influence of the systemic field goes beyond illusion questions. I'm quite inspired by the idea that relationships and interactions within a system are bigger than the sum of the individual parts, especially how this relates to leadership[11]. The miracle question often goes something like this: *"Imagine a miracle happened and your problem was solved. How would you know?"* and is just one of many in the field of Solution-Focused Brief Therapy[12].

When we ask these types of questions, we are asking about the properties of the solution, observable in the real world. This constrains the solution, as all of a sudden we have a specific property to take into account, and we are, in essence, now converging instead of diverging.

Most business professionals know about The Theory of Constraints from the book The Goal[13], which talks about constraints as something that is limiting flow and must be removed.

ENABLING CONSTRAINTS IS SOMETHING ELSE. THEY PROMOTE FLOW AND PROGRESS, AND WE ARE BETTER OFF FOR HAVING THEM.

The illusion questions essentially elicit enabling constraints. For example, the rumble strips on the road constrain us from driving off the road and avoiding accidents. A conductor is a constraint, keeping the orchestra from going off-beat. Neither of those constraints should be removed. On the contrary, they enable progress. Hence, they are very different from The Theory of Constraints. This, by the way, does not suggest that The Theory of Constraints is a bad thing. On the contrary, The Goal is a wonderful book with a lot of great advice if you work in a predictable environment.

Constraints can be soft and undefinable, like cultural taboos. If you know that there are topics that will make people uncomfortable to talk about, a taboo can be an enabling constraint.

This could initially read like design thinking[14] or the double diamond process[15], but there's a difference. A double-diamond process is a single loop of generating ideas and converging toward a solution. Working with illusion questions and the magical process is a series of loops, incorporating feedback at every loop.

An illusion question seems simple when read without context but serves a dedicated purpose. By asking questions regarding things specifically observable in the real world, we can help the transition from imagination to reality by adding enabling constraints. You are directing the focus toward the object by asking about *modalities*.

The concept is to think about your questions. Could they be answered in the imaginary world?

LET'S EXPLORE THE USE OF MODALITIES IN ILLUSION QUESTIONS

"How do you know that?" is an illusion question. It differs from a "why" question because it elicits reality responses.

In the context of magic:
"The coin vanished from his hand!" says the spectator.

"How do you know that?"

"I saw the coin, and then it was gone!"

"Did you see heads or tails?"

"Uhm.."

"Did the light reflect in the coin?"

"Uhm.. maybe I did not see it directly, but I'm sure it was there."

While those questions might seem banal, notice how they inquire about real modalities. A modality refers to how information is presented or expressed, for instance, visual, auditory, tactile, etc.

If the spectator witnessed an illusion, the brain wouldn't, nor could it, spend capacity on whether the head or tail side of the coin was visible.

That is what the illusion question does for you. They help move something from imagination into reality. If we didn't have illusion questions, we would end up with solutions that only work in the imaginary world, rendering them useless.

IN THE CONTEXT OF LEADERSHIP:

"Joshua hates me," says Kim. You respond with an illusion question, eliciting something real from the statement:

"How do you know that?" you ask, gently moving toward reality by asking about the modality of the statement.

"He says mean things about me," Kim says, staying in what could be imagined. We don't know if this is real or imagined, so we ask another question about reality:

"What specifically have you heard him say?". Notice how we are asking for real modalities.

"Well, he says things about me behind my back," Kim answers.

"How do you know that?" You continue, gently moving away from imagination and into reality.

A question on a belief will often open up a debate on observable behaviors. Instead of asking the same question, you can make variations:

"Why does *this* mean *that*." Often used either as *"This causes that"* or *"This means That,"* and often as a limiting belief. *"I don't have an MBA, so I will not be a good leader."* Look for "so" or "therefore" or other words that equate two sentences. Asking specifically why A means B creates a structure for the conversation that enables the person to see the reality part. Often, the limitations people see are apparent in the imaginary world, but when you ask for them to be described in the real world, they diminish.

Other words to listen for are "must," "have," "should," etc. They imply that the person saying that does not feel like they have a choice.

"I must keep Joshua on the team," says Kim, and as you notice the must, it triggers you to ask:

"What would happen if you didn't?"

Often, people can be stuck in a limiting belief, and "must" is one of those words that can be challenged.

Sometimes, people bring only the conviction of a belief from imagination to reality, and an illusion question to deal with that could be, *"If you were to teach me, how would you do that?"*

"I am terrible at public speaking, which makes me nervous."

"If you were to teach me how to be bad at public speaking and nervous, how would you do that?"

Suddenly, the problem is detached from the person, who is no longer a victim but rather an expert. This structure lets you move the issue back to the imagination, having almost silly conversations. Remember that "illusion" means "to play with," so it is okay that it is a bit silly – it is playing, after all.

Once your team is accustomed to Illusion questions, you can get exceptional results by bypassing limiting beliefs. I often got good results with the following, much to the surprise – and pleasure – of the person I am coaching.

Let's say the dialogue is at a point where the person says: "I don't know."

And, without pausing a beat, you ask:

"WHAT WOULD THE ANSWER BE IF YOU DID KNOW?"

It reads like a trick question but is almost magical when it works. You will be surprised when a person who just said "I don't know" comes up with a potential solution just because you asked that question.

The more illusion questions you ask, the more you learn. But is learning inherently valuable or just nice to have? Let's take a look at how I define the learning organization.

SCHOOL'S OUT

The power of
LEARNING

As with any other profession, each magician has their own view points, and there are more subjects on which we disagree than we agree. I am sure there will be magicians reading this book, yelling at the pages that they would have done something differently. One thing on which we can all agree, though, is that our tricks, effects, and narrative are improved through constant learning and that learning comes through feedback.

Table-hopping is a specific branch of close-up magic. It is when you walk from table to table at a restaurant, performing for people in between courses. I did a lot of table-hopping in my days as a close-up magician. It was the perfect entertainment at corporate parties. I had three sets of close-up tricks, so if a table looked at the neighboring table, they would still see something new. After a whole night of table-hopping, even with three different sets, I would have performed the same trick multiple times, and this was what eventually made me a skilled magician.

It wasn't talent or that I was particularly gifted in any way. It was the enormous amount of feedback I received every weekend. It didn't matter if the feedback was positive or negative; it was filled with valuable insights. Each comment, laugh, or reaction was taken in as feedback. If a particular sequence received good feedback, I would increase that sequence. If a part of the set did not get good reactions, I would decrease whatever I did in that segment.

Jokes and funny tidbits would evolve, often based on something a spectator was saying. The whole set was organic, constantly receiving feedback that was instantly incorporated and tried out at the following table. This meant that a small change could evolve into a big change during the night. I would change words, tonality, body language, pauses, stances, you name it. Everything that could elicit feedback could be improved.

It is an evolutionary improvement, with each generation taking place in the space of minutes.

IN THE EARLY DAYS, I CALLED THIS EVOLUTIONARY LEARNING.

Evolutionary Learning is now more typically associated with AI and neural networks, where you can simulate a lot of generations in a very short period of time. The same learning patterns that happen in evolution are happening here; only we are creating the space for this to happen quickly and often.

When I first brought this behavior from entertainment into the business, it raised some eyebrows. Back then, it was customary to have a yearly feedback session between the leader and the employee. "Year-end feedback" or "Employee Development Conversation" and the like were popular. The employee would get feedback on the performance during the year that had passed and talk about development areas for the year to come.

My leadership peers shook their heads when I talked about continuous feedback, so to begin with, I applied it to my own learning. I considered every interaction, dialogue, and criticism a learning opportunity. That approach accomplished several different outcomes. First and foremost, it enabled me to learn quickly and incorporate what I have learned into my daily work. Secondly, my attitude facing criticism had an unexpected side effect. As I yearned for feedback, my colleagues would see me listen carefully and be interested, even when the other person was criticizing. This behavior shaped my narrative as a leader, always holding my head up straight.

ALMOST ANY INTERACTION BRINGS LEARNING. I EITHER CREATE, RETAIN, OR TRANSFER KNOWLEDGE.

Each of these brings something to the organization and to me. I quickly became comfortable enough to lean into the learning mindset and ignore the idea of annual feedback and began a habit of continuous feedback. Soon after, I wanted to pursue the concept of organizational learning, not just personal learning.

I had read "The Fifth Discipline[16]", which was – and is – very influential when it comes to organizational learning. I was building on that idea but wanted more than continuous improvement. I wanted to produce knowledge. I wanted the organization to retain what it learned. I wanted an organization where transferring knowledge was second nature.

Continuous improvement can, on its own, be counterproductive. Think of it like the tiny adjustments to the flight control surfaces you might see on the wings of a jet plane. A small dip of one on the left wing makes the plane change direction slightly to the right. This ensures that the plane reaches the exact destination, saving fuel and time. However, what if it was the wrong destination? Or what if flying was the wrong means of transportation? Maybe the train would have been better. Or maybe we shouldn't even go east. Or maybe we shouldn't even travel; we should grow potatoes. I have seen many a great department optimizing via continuous improvement towards a wrong goal. Without *double-loop learning*[17], there is no learning at all.

Double-loop learning is a concept in organizational learning that refers to the process of questioning and challenging the underlying assumptions that guide an organization's actions. It involves going beyond simply adjusting one's actions to achieve a desired outcome and instead involves a more fundamental reevaluation of the goals and assumptions that guide those actions.

To my surprise, the biggest obstacle in introducing double-loop thinking was leadership—or, rather, leaders. I remember the first session I did. The feedback I got was that the employees felt they were disobeying me by questioning the direction I had set earlier. The whole session became too "polite" in a way. As the leader, I was associated with the directions, meaning any challenge to that, was seen as a challenge to me.

That Friday, at the weekly magic gig, I tried something different while table-hopping. My appearance as a magician was nice and charming, and my spectators rarely challenged me. I wanted to elicit that challenge, so I changed a few things in my storyline.

I asked a spectator to pick a card, any card. I held up the card and said: *"Notice, the cards are not marked on the back side. They are also not marked on the face, so I have no idea which card you selected".* As I said those words, I was at first pointing at the back side of the card, then I turned it over and pointed at the face of the card. It was obvious that I was looking right at the card and knew exactly what card they had picked.

The funny thing is that even then, the spectators were nodding as I said: *"I have no idea what card you picked."* I had to clearly say, *"Ok, time out – you do realize I'm staring right at the card!?"* Only at that point did it get a laugh, and the next time I did a less-so-obvious peek at a card, they called me out on it. Great, I had gotten what I wanted. Now how could I bring that attitude back to the professional world?

Back in the office, I celebrated when people asked questions about our strategic direction and core beliefs. I wanted to demonstrate that this was acceptable behavior and that there were no stupid questions.

YOU'RE NOT IGNORANT FOR ASKING QUESTIONS.

ADMITTING A MISTAKE IS A SIGN OF STRENGTH, NOT INCOMPETENCE.

OFFERING NEW IDEAS IS CATERING TO INNOVATION, NOT BEING INTRUSIVE.

And most importantly, critique is a gift you give others to learn; it is not negative in any way, shape, or form.

As I was getting the organization comfortable with double-loop learning, I still had work to do on transferring knowledge before I was happy with calling my organization a learning organization. You could argue that transferring knowledge is teaching, not learning, but I'll take that.

Shifting state again, back to being a magician. Most magicians have something at which they excel, and very few excel at everything. If I want to improve my coin palming, I know exactly who is best at palming coins and whom I could contact. I know whom to call if I want to learn a new card side steal. Magic is quite multi-faceted, and while some may have very good finger dexterity to do sleight of hand, others can memorize a deck of cards in 10 seconds. Some may be great wordsmiths and can create captivating storylines, while others may have a "funny bone", and almost everything they say seems to be funny. No one told them to be specialists in this area – they chose based on skill, capabilities, or interest. That inspired me to change the way our teams worked.

In the business world at the time, it was customary to move people to work. You would get a project, assemble a project team, and the people went on to new projects once the project was done. While that model had proven to work for many years, I found that it did not cater to learning. Sure, most project models had after-action reviews and post-mortems, but I had some issues with those. First, the learning was done after the project was finished, whereas I would prefer continuous learning throughout the project and beyond. Secondly, no one ever read any of those AAR reports. After a while, people would forget the knowledge hidden in those reports.

Here's what I did instead.

AN ORGANIZATION THAT IS LEARNING – THE FOUR RULES

First, I made the rule that a team was the smallest logical unit in terms of capacity planning. Until then, we had spent more hours than I care to remember discussing FTEs (Full Time Employees) and matching capacity to work in terms of people. We had done so because that's how the rest of the business did capacity planning, but no one had made the double loop of asking, "Why?".

So, I changed that.

Second, teams are stable and long-lived capability teams. Instead of assembling and disassembling teams, teams can now stay together. The team decides on what capability/capabilities they would like to be known for and commits to helping other teams on that subject. Knowledge capturing is more than documentation; it is also the tacit knowledge built in a stable team. By being the experts on a topic, the team members naturally gravitate towards acquiring knowledge of the topic, and by sharing, they increase their capability and become subject matter experts.

Third, work is flowing to teams. No more moving people between projects. Any product is based on a mix of capabilities. Any given value stream requires a capability mix, and the stable, long-lived capability teams align towards a value stream. This solidifies the stable team setup and ensures that the cognitive load of a team doesn't get too high to handle. Since the value stream has all the capabilities needed to deliver, there are no handovers and, therefore, no need for project management, no dependencies, and thus fast flow and optimal learning.

Fourth, finally – and most important of all – the primary objective of a team is to learn. This principle is the one most frequently frowned upon by leadership peers. Surely, the primary goal of a team is to deliver value first and foremost? Well, yes – but how do you know you deliver optimal value without learning?

Just like the close-up magic set evolves with every feedback loop, so does the product.

THE FASTER YOU LEARN, AND THE QUICKER YOU CAN INTEGRATE THOSE INSIGHTS INTO THE PRODUCT, THE MORE VALUE IS CREATED.

If you just keep your nose to the grindstone, you will produce what you originally planned, but unless you are creating a commodity that has been done many times before, you will get smarter during the process and learn new and valuable things about your product. This is the core difference between the agile approach and the waterfall approach. In waterfall, you know everything upfront and can write requirement specifications. If what you are working on is not a commodity but something that has not been done before, you don't know the exact requirements upfront. In agile, you only know the outcome you want to achieve, not the output that will generate that outcome, so you work in short feedback loops, embracing change to the requirements. As you create the solution, you learn new things about your market, technology landscape, customers, etc. This learning is fed back into the process through the learning loops, creating a better and stronger end product. Henceforth, learning is prioritized higher than delivering.

These four choices are the ones that I made to create an "organization that is learning". The reasons for not calling this "a learning organization" are that it differs from Peter Senge's definition, and the outcomes differ.

This example is from my time in the LEGO Group, which is my most recent work on creating an organization that is learning and the work I am most proud of. I made attempts before in previous jobs, but not nearly as successful, as I hadn't clarified the benefits of learning to myself and my organization. In short, here are the five bullet points of learning that may inspire you.

THE FIVE PRINCIPLES OF LEARNING

Learning creates better outcomes. Short feedback loops create a better end product if you work with wicked problems. That is, a problem that does not have a definite answer but only can be "better" or "worse". Solving a Rubik's cube is not wicked because it has a definite answer. It is either solved or not solved. Treating a patient, teaching a student, and building a social media app are all wicked. You are never done, but the outcome can become better or worse, and feedback loops are key drivers.

Learning creates capacity. The more knowledge a team acquires, the more work can flow through this team without asking for help from other teams. This means you might not need an extra team because the capabilities can be found in existing teams because they have learned them.

Learning creates flow. The more a team knows, the fewer dependencies are created. Dependencies are the biggest impediment to flow, and with fewer dependencies, work flows faster. This does not mean that teams work harder or longer hours. On the contrary, this means teams can focus on teamwork with a reduced need for collaboration. While collaboration is often praised as a positive (because it most often is), it is also something that has a price in terms of cognitive load. If you collaborate with another team, you must understand that other team.

Learning increases quality. When teams are accountable for the entire value stream, they also own the quality of the outcome. As opposed to a car manufacturer, where a product goes through different stages, and quality assurance is a stage at the end, a learning team has quality assurance built into their processes instead of relying on a separate team.

Learning increases motivation. Traditionally, companies try to motivate teams with incentives, giving them money, perks, or bonuses. However, intrinsic motivation is like love and cannot be bought. The learning organization is for knowledge workers, and people working with knowledge are motivated by learning and sharing knowledge. Being accountable for the outcome as a team increases pride in the work and further increases intrinsic motivation.

The described principles work if your product or service is complex. If your product or service is something that can be completely described before the work is started, and the output is guaranteed if you follow the procedure, then this process is not recommended. Continuous improvement is a good thing if the output is consistent. The root-cause analysis and standardization of work will benefit anything repeatable. A car manufacturing plant will benefit highly because each car should preferably be like the previous one.

However, if what you are doing differs between subjects, there is probably never a single root cause and a one-size-fits-all model will be counterproductive in a complex area.

But how do you know if what you are doing is, in fact, complex? Let's take a deep dive into the fascinating land of complexity theory, explained in simple terms with many examples.

INTER-
LUDE

A novel approach to complexity
science and how it enables us to navigate

UNCERTAINTY AND AMBIGUITY

I have come to realize at this point that we are about to dive into the tangled arena of complexity. We will redefine it through one of my more unashamed and beloved "nerdisms". And because I really don't want to lose anyone here – as this is when we make a brief but vital foray into the world of natural science – I would like to point out that it is included because not only is it fascinating, but it is also important to the trip we are taking just as a stout pair of walking boots are to a successful hike in the mountains.

Never fear; the gradient at the start is not so steep. You might feel slightly flummoxed initially, but I promise you will be enlightened at the end of the chapter.

Our journey begins in ancient Greece, where Heron of Alexandria lived at the end of the first century. He was a Greek mathematician and engineer and is relatively unknown, even though he invented the steam engine[18] and the vending machine[19].

At some point, he became interested in frustums. Or rather, he became interested in the math behind frustums – a pyramid with the top cut off.

As Heron was doing calculations on frustums, he stumbled upon something strange. The square root of negative numbers.

Not only were negative numbers new to him – *"How can I have minus two tomatoes? I can't imagine that."* – but the idea of taking the square root of a negative number was unthinkable. If he had continued down that path, accepting these imaginary numbers, a real solution could have been found. Had he followed the line of thought described in the previous chapter, just accepting parts of the equation as impossible, he might have solved it, as his math up until then checks out. Little did he know that he had stumbled upon complex numbers, and his line of calculations was correct.

Years later, the French philosopher René Descartes left his fingerprints on these strange numbers. Descartes was a philosopher primarily known for his *"Cogito, Ergo Sum"* – *"I think therefore I am."* He was working on an appendix to a book on discourse called "La

Géométrie" in which he names these strange numbers *"imaginary."* The fact that it was Descartes that coined the term "imaginary" is maybe not so strange once you realize that he never actually said, *"I think therefore I am."*

Descartes imagined an "evil demon[20]" (sometimes referred to as Descartes' demon) that could create an illusion of reality. How will we know that we are not living in an artificial space created by this demon? This idea is explored in the 1999 movie *The Matrix*, where citizens think they live a normal life, yet they are all living in a giant computer simulation.

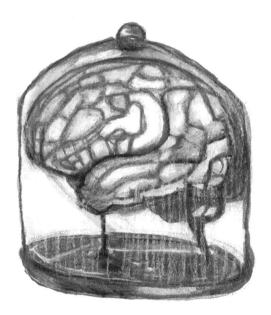

Descartes was questioning how you know you are not just a brain in a vat on the desk of an evil scientist, and he began to doubt his own existence. But this doubt, he realized, is what proves that he exists. So, he wrote, *"I doubt, therefore I am"*, or as we have come to know it: *"I think, therefore I am"*. Being a Frenchman, the actual words he wrote in 1637 were: *"Je pense, donc je suis."*. This was later translated as *"I think,*

therefore I am," but understanding what it was that Descartes was really trying to work out here, the correct translation probably should have been *"I am thinking, therefore I am."* The active act of doubting, or thinking, whether or not you exist, presupposes that you are not just an imagination.

The influence of Descartes in the section on illusion questions is perhaps obvious. By asking questions that presuppose reality, we transcend into existence, and it makes sense that he was the one to coin the imaginary part of complexity.

While we know who coined the term "imaginary," we don't know for sure whom we should credit for discovering imaginary numbers. The reason for this is so marvelously interesting that it will probably be made into a movie at some point.

WHO KNEW THAT THE SECRETS OF MATHEMATICS WERE ONCE GUARDED MORE CLOSELY THAN THE SECRETS OF MAGIC?

Mathematical secrets were used as weapons and used in duels that endangered the duelant's livelihood.

In the 16th century, knowledge of imaginary numbers was a secret weapon. Back in those days, you didn't apply for a job as a mathematician by submitting your resume. You challenged the incumbent in the role you were after to a duel. Instead of crossing swords, you would exchange questions with each other, with the one answering the most questions emerging victorious – and landing the job.

Thus, possessing a mathematical secret could both save your livelihood and give you job security. Imaginary numbers were one such secret, and one so closely guarded that it wasn't written down, and people would literally take the secret with them to the grave.

Back then, math was closely linked to reality – it was even an expression of it. It was used to calculate land, buildings, goods for trade, profits, etc. Math describes something tangible. You would use it to calculate the amount of rice in a barrel, and it was far from the theoretical matter it is today. Formulas were a thing, but math equations were often described in pictures. Solving a second-degree equation – a quadratic equation – was depicted as squares with an area. Not only did this make it tangible to calculate, but it also helped teach math, as the visual part was easy to understand. A square with a side length of x had the area x^2. This was all good and easy to understand, and the solution to quadratic equations had been known for ages. Farmers used quadratic equations to calculate how many acres of land they had and could easily connect math with reality.

It was also well established that there were no solutions to third-degree equations – cubic equations. Leonardo da Vinci's math teacher – Luca Pacioli – wrote in 1494 that, contrary to the quadratic equation, no general formula could be found for the cubic equations[21]. It was so hard to understand because of the connection to reality, and here's why:

If you remember your algebra (who doesn't?), solving these is by "completing the cube". That is, adding a cube and removing it again later, like the Camel principle. It looks easy in writing, but mathematicians had difficulty drawing – or even imagining – a cube with a negative volume. The only way to solve the cubic equation was to remove math from reality and transport it into the imaginary – to be comfortable with taking the square root of negative numbers.

SOME FOUND OUT HOW TO IMAGINE A CUBE WITH A NEGATIVE VOLUME AND USED THAT SECRET FOR WEALTH AND TASTE, DESTROYING THEIR COUNTERPARTS IN DUELS OF WIT.

The history of imaginary numbers reads like a Dan Brown novel – only in this case it's true. Secrets were kept in poems, riddles, or curious pictures. This means that if you know at least a little about what you are looking for, you'll find it well documented through letters sent between the dueling mathematicians. That said, a single, unique source for imagining these numbers is nigh on impossible to identify. But having read through a lot of the material, I would give honorable mentions to Scipione del Ferro, Niccolò Fontana Tartaglia, Gerolamo Cardano, and Rafael Bombelli.

IF HISTORY AND MATH INTEREST YOU, I WOULD URGE YOU TO LOOK UP THE FANTASTIC STORY BEHIND THE INCREDIBLE DUELS AND FIGHTS THESE GENIUSES HAD – NOT WITH WEAPONS BUT WITH PEN AND PAPER – AND MINDS.

The secret they all fought over was about how to solve a problem by adding imagination.

LATER, THE COMBINATION OF REALITY AND IMAGINATION WAS NAMED "COMPLEX."

A complex number is the sum of a real and an imaginary number. Many people have been credited for coining the term "complex," including Caspar Wessel and Carl Friedrich Gauss.

In mathematics, it might seem strange to call numbers "real," "imaginary," and "complex," as all are very real in the realm of mathematics, but the nomenclature stuck, so we will use it here as well.

A whole field of complexity science exists, which takes a more granular view of the area. We are taking a slightly different route here, so if you are familiar with other frameworks, you will see some differences and some similarities.

For us to generalize the concepts and make them more useful, let's take a moment to familiarize ourselves with how to categorize complex issues in the context of this book.

IS THIS THE REAL LIFE? IS THIS JUST FANTASY?

BOHEMIAN RHAP- SODY

How different parts compose
A BEAUTIFUL SONG

A COMPLEX ISSUE IS SOMETHING THAT CANNOT BE EASILY EXPLAINED. **IT HAS REAL AND IMAGINARY COMPONENTS.** IT IS NOT COMPLEX IF YOU CAN WRITE A MANUAL DESCRIBING EVERY STEP. THAT'S WHY A CAR IS NOT COMPLEX – YOU CAN DISASSEMBLE A CAR AND HAVE SOMEONE ELSE ASSEMBLE IT, AND IT WILL WORK IMMEDIATELY. BUT TRAFFIC IN A BUSY CITY IS COMPLEX.

Traffic is the sum of many independent agents, and the sum is bigger than the parts. A car slowing down or a pedestrian stumbling when crossing the road will cause ripples in the traffic that are impossible to predict. And if the same car slows down at the same time tomorrow, something completely different could happen.

Getting married is not complex, but having a happy marriage is. There is a manual for getting married, and several people can follow the manual, resulting in legal matrimony. But there is no "best practice" for a happy marriage. You cannot follow a manual or copy someone else's relationship. A happy marriage is the sum of many small parts, which is impossible to predict.

Building the Taj Mahal out of LEGO bricks is not complex. You do not need to try several different approaches; you can simply follow the instructions. There is a best practice, and the whole equals the sum of the parts.

Raising a teenager is complex. There is no best practice; you cannot copy someone else's work, expecting the same results.

Leadership in complexity calls for something other than plans and best practices. It's not linear; it is cyclic.

The process resembles the method scientists have used since at least the 17th century. It is a cyclical process that constantly refines a conclusion. There's evidence that this method works just as well in business as in science[22].

The scientific method is in itself easy to understand: You begin with an observation or a question. A hypothesis can be created after researching the topic area, which can then be tested experimentally. The data from the test is then observed, and a new cycle begins until a satisfactory result remains.

Sense what is happening. Find a source of input and get some data.

Decide on a small action based on the data.

Respond with that action and observe the results.

Learn from the reaction and start another loop.

A simple example is a chef in need of a new starter dish. The chef might decide it should be based on bread and research various forms of spicy sourdough bread. How much spice and how many are still unknown, so let's bake a few and try them out. Get feedback by observing the people eating the bread and listening to what they say. Adjust the recipe based on the feedback, rinse, and repeat.

There's a loop around the loop, though. The initial decision was that it should be based on bread. How do we know if a seafood salad wouldn't have been better?

And there is a loop around that as well. How do you know that the customer experience will be better by changing the starter dish? Maybe money would be better spent on new chairs or better music.

How do we handle all that complexity? How do we move from complexity to reality? What leadership behaviors should we focus on when facing a complex problem?

A real solution is something tangible that answers a complex problem. Example:

"A chair" is the answer to "I would like to sit comfortably".

But the answer might just as well be "a Fatboy®" or "a chaise longue".

THE FIRST THING TO DO WHEN WORKING IN COMPLEXITY IS TO HAVE THE QUESTION PHRASED AT THE RIGHT LEVEL. IT HAS TO BE UP TO THE IMAGINATION HOW TO SOLVE IT, SO EXPRESS THE QUESTION WITH ONLY THE IMAGINARY PART.

Don't say "Build me a car" when the need being answered is "how can I be transported from A to B". Don't say "Build me a boat" when the question is "How do I cross the river" as "Build me a bridge" is also a suitable answer.

Asking the right question is essential, and a guiding principle is to ask the question in the imaginary world, not the real world. A litmus test for asking the right question is if the question only has one answer. "I would like to sit comfortably" has several answers. "Build me a chair" only has one response. This is what can transform a simple song into a rhapsody.

ASK ABOUT THE OUTCOME, NOT THE OUTPUT.

What is it that you want to achieve? Leave the "how" for later, when it is transformed into the real world.

A famous example is John F. Kennedy, who on May 25th 1961 in his address to Congress famously said: *"I believe that this nation should commit itself to achieving the goal, before this decade is out, of landing a man on the moon and returning him safely to the earth."* Notice how the entire statement is imaginary – he does not mention spaceships, propulsion engines, or anything that made this real. He simply put the desired outcome into words.

As Albert Einstein famously never said: *"A problem cannot be solved at the same level used to create it."*

A few years ago, I heard about someone who wanted to get people to eat more vegetarian food, as they firmly believed it would be better for the planet. Now that's a complex question.

They initially experimented by creating an app with recipes from the world's finest chefs. The app should make it easy for people to get the right ingredients and cook the perfect meal. However, as they listened to the feedback from the users, it was often a problem to have the time to shop in between picking kids up from school, doing homework, driving them to soccer practice, family time, and so forth.

The team, sticking to their original question, created a new hypothesis. Maybe they would reach the outcome by bringing food to the customers' homes, thus saving them time. They would do all the initial preparation, so the customers only needed to put the final touches on the meal, which would be ready to eat. As that turned out to be a success, they could now move the problem out of complexity and start improving their new business line, transforming from an app development company to a food and logistics company.

The framing of a complex question enabled them to make loops within loops until reaching something that could be transformed and is now a reality and a successful business. If the company seems to stagnate or decline at some point, it is always possible to move it back into the realm of imagination and reimagine something else.

Consider the leadership needed in complexity. Most of our leadership body of knowledge comes from the industrial age and is – more or less – based on the idea of Scientific Management that Fredric Taylor proposed around the turn of the last century[23]. It works well for problems that are not complex. As we saw above, a car is not complex, but traffic is. The car industry is a perfect example of a very well-tuned machine, and great tools and techniques were born out of the automobile industry. However, all the analysis, plans, and LEAN methodologies, which are great for building a car, are useless if your problem is traffic.

The issue with traffic is not the cars, the buses, the bicycles, or the pedestrians. It is in the relationship between them. A vehicle making a wrong turn on Monday morning will result in a completely different scenario than the same car making the same turn at the same place on another day. The problem "lives in the aether" between the agents.

The elements of a complex system are autonomous agents interacting with each other, constantly trying to learn from what is happening. The car that took a wrong turn can turn back into the lane, but the effects of the action have already started. There is no causality or reversibility. When we see a bird's eye view of a busy part of town, it looks like some collective behavior is occurring. Not unlike what we see when we look at a flock of birds, an ant colony, or a school of fish. They appear to move as one, yet we are in no doubt that they are separate entities. Yet these systems can be so closely coupled together that they look like a single entity. Like the Portuguese man o'war – It looks like a jellyfish, but it is made up of many small individual organisms called zooids.

More and more of the problems modern business leaders face are complex. If you work as a stockbroker and look at the stock market, you will see the same patterns described above. Small changes, like a wrong word uttered at a press conference, can change stock prices. If you are the dean of a school, looking at the dynamics of the students, you will recognize the same patterns. Complexity is in every branch of business, whether you work in healthcare or create digital solutions. Whenever you are working with people, you have complexity. Managing the "aether" is different from managing the individual agents. **Understanding this as a leader will open up a magical world, and you will sometimes feel like a magician when you see your "flock of birds" reacting to your leadership.**

WHEN MANAGING COMPLEXITY, IT IS ESSENTIAL TO ACKNOWLEDGE THAT THERE IS NO "YES/NO" ANSWER.

Whether leading a business, raising a teenager, working in healthcare, or building a product, you would never say, "ok – I'm done." **You are never "done" with a complex problem.** You can make it better or worse, but it's never done. Imagine someone saying, *"ok, we're done inventing the computer."* There is more computer power in the phone you have in your pocket than there was behind the Apollo 11 landing on the moon. The computer has improved significantly and will probably continue to do so. It's not done. Traditional project management tracking is impossible without a deadline or clear "definition of done." Thus, trying to manage complex projects with conventional project management tools will do more harm than good.

Instead, consider the loops within the loops analogy. Make a hypothesis that *"this will improve the product, and this is how I can measure it."* Conduct an experiment that will validate this. Increase what works, dampen what doesn't work. Remember the outer loops; do not get caught up in optimizing just one thing. Maybe it is not a better camera that the smartphone needs to increase market share, so remember to think of new answers to the original complex problem.

Notice that data is data. If you launch a prototype and it "fails," then that is just as valuable as if you had succeeded.

SOMETIMES, WE MIGHT EVEN LEARN MORE FROM A FAILED HYPOTHESIS BECAUSE WHEN WE FACE THE UNEXPECTED, WE OFTEN STOP AND SCRATCH OUR HEADS, WONDERING HOW THAT HAPPENED.

Some scientific studies tell us that unexpected results also make us remember them better[24]. There is nothing wrong with failure from a learning and development point of view as long as we use the data.

When something is improved, it is always based on what it was and how it is now. Just like a complex number is comprised the same way as a vector – something with a direction and a velocity, we measure how fast things are going in the right direction.

THERE ARE NO FIXED KPIS IN THE COMPLEX DOMAIN.

If you are leading a hospital, chasing a specific number for the patient's blood pressure or glucose levels makes little sense. They are all individuals, and progress is based on what it was and how it is now. Better or worse.

This is especially relevant for those of you doing digital solutions. Be aware that if humans use your solutions, they are complex, and chasing a number will almost always be counterproductive. Try to find a vector instead of a number. How do we know that we have improved something, and how well are we improving? Always look at measurements from the perspective of the user/customer/citizen. Ideally, combine quantitative and qualitative data. Just because the number of calls is decreasing at the call center, does that mean happy customers? Talk to the users and include stories in the measurement of success.

Looking at improvements as relative is almost instantly recognized as something positive, yet it is rarely realized. The number one reason why this is not happening is a result of performance being linked to incentive plans. There is still a belief among some leaders that incentives drive behavior, and you will see incentive plans and bonus agreements for complex systems based on specific numbers. While this is easy to manage, it creates an unhealthy system. You can only do that with systems that are not complex – where the whole is the sum of the parts, and there is clear causality.

You may want to move as much of the problem as possible into reality. Some parts of a problem might be realized through analysis, planning, and execution. These parts can be "done." You can't say when you will have a happy marriage, but you can take the wedding ceremony into reality and say when you are legally married. You can't know when your hospital is done, but you can take the problem of removing the appendix of a single patient and make it real. You know how to do it, and there is a clear "definition of done." There are well-educated experts who understand the cause and effects of actions taken.

SINCE THERE IS NO CAUSE AND EFFECT IN THE COMPLEX SPACE, THE EXPERTS ONLY COME INTO PLAY WHEN YOU REALIZE A PROBLEM, SO IT IS A GOOD WAY TO ENGAGE THE EXPERTISE OF THE SYSTEM.

Now is also the time to bring out the time-tested methods of Taylor's scientific management. If a problem is no longer complex, you can measure specifics, make continuous improvements, and implement KPIs. This is also where you can employ 'best practice.' If the experts are there and the solution to a problem can be repeated with the same result, 'best practice' is a wonderful tool.

SIMPLICITY AND CLARITY ARE NOT GOALS. FORCING SIMPLICITY OR CLARITY IS A LOGICAL FALLACY KNOWN AS CAUSAL REDUCTIONISM.

The fallacy is easy to fall for – otherwise, it wouldn't be a fallacy. You will see many a business with "traditional" leadership praising the dashboard. The cockpit demonstrating how the entire business is running. While this is a strong and meaningful tool if you have known problems and established methods, it is counter-productive when working with complex problems.

Studies show that the culprit is us[25]. Humans. We prefer to do business in an environment with a simple cause and effect, where the whole is the sum of the parts, and you can make detailed plans for the future.

Who can blame us, though? Life would be easier without complexity, and the desire to simplify is evident. We would feel in control if we could reduce our entire business to a metrics dashboard. We would be happy when the lights are green and know when to take action if the lights are red. The problem is that any complex problem lives in the aether – that part of the universe that exists beyond our tangible reality. You can measure the individual parts to your heart's content, but that would be missing the actual facts altogether. Not only does it give the wrong picture, but it also creates unwanted behavior.

These types of problems – problems that cannot be solved, but only get better or worse – are called **Wicked Problems**[26]. I have written more about Wicked Problems in my book "Wonderful Digital Leadership[27]".

The thing with tangible metrics is that there is causality. You can change something (the cause), and the metric will move (the effect). In complexity, there is no cause and effect.

Imagine a complex problem: The city of Howfarawayville would like more tourists. A lot of parameters influence the influx of tourism. Someone suggests that fewer rats will cause more tourists. The city starts to measure the number of killed rats and even incentivizes the citizens to kill rats. Citizens start to breed rats and show up with boxes of dead rats, improving the metric. The city officials learn about the breeding and stop the measurement and incentive plan. The citizens release all the rats they'd been breeding because they are now worthless. The number of rats is now bigger than it was before. While this example is made up[28], chances are you can think of real examples – maybe even from your current organization. In their 2022 book, "Limits of the numerical: the abuses and uses of quantification[29]", Newfield et al writes: *"Numbers are both controlling and fragile. At the same time, they are frequent objects of obfuscation, manipulation, or outright denial. Numbers presuppose categories which themselves encode worldviews and histories."*

NO 'BEST PRACTICE' EXISTS IN THE COMPLEX SPACE BECAUSE NO TWO PROBLEMS ARE ALIKE.

That is why it makes little sense to copy what another organization is doing and expect the same results[30]. It is just as meaningless as copying the actions of a happy couple and expecting a happy marriage. As a leader, I often see presentations suggesting, "Successful companies do this. Therefore, we should do it as well". The thing is that unsuccessful companies often use the same methods as successful ones. You cannot copy the actions done in the complex space, but you can in the real space, as long as you are aware of "the survivorship bias."

Down the road from where we live is a lovely old house. It is several hundred years old, and whenever people walk past it, they often say: **"They don't make them like they used to do."** You have probably heard this said about a plentiful of things: an old chair or a vintage car. It is an example of "survivorship bias." We don't see the houses, cars, or chairs that have perished. We only see the ones that still exist.

When we see successful companies that used a specific method or process, we don't see the failed companies that used the exact same method or process. You may have heard about the story of the WWII airplanes and the bullet holes. When the planes returned from a mission, they looked at where the bullet had hit the plane. They found that it was almost always the same place and decided to reinforce those parts of the aircraft. That is until the mathematician Abraham Wald[1] famously never said: "You should reinforce those parts **without** bullet holes. These aircraft survived with the damage – those that were hit the other places didn't survive and did not return home."

[1]Abraham Wald was a mathematician and a member of the Statistical Research Group during WWII. His work was influential, but the stories about his work have simplified it beyond recognition in popular internet culture.

The planes that survived the shootings are not as important as the ones that did not survive—an excellent example of survivorship bias.

I have witnessed survivorship bias repeatedly among senior leaders in small and big companies, and it is easy to understand why it prevails. Reading about other companies' successes and believing that copying what they do will somehow make your own company successful is a soothing thought for a senior executive under pressure from shareholders, boards, and customers. Several books embracing the success narratives reach the bestseller lists. The 1982 bestseller "In Search of Excellence" sold millions of copies in its first years. This is why your company probably has "bias for action" somewhere in its strategic documents, as that was one of the eight shared properties of successful companies, according to the book. Later, we saw the rise of the 2001 bestseller "Good to Great,[31]" which presents the reader with seven properties that successful companies have in common. While these are all great books, they lure the reader into the trap of success narratives and survivorship bias. If you are curious about this, several scientific articles explore this subject, for instance, the 2021 article "Success stories cause false beliefs about success[32]."

Hopefully, I have given enough examples in this chapter of complex problems so that you can know when to apply what kind of leadership. At the very least, I hope I have sparked your curiosity.

The next chapter explores why I believe curiosity is an important leadership muscle that, as much as any other muscle, needs regular exercise. Especially if you work in a field where innovation is key for the success and sustainability of the company.

ALL ALONG THE WATCH- TOWER

How a tale of magic rabbits will change your view on

INNOVATION

Back in 1895, in a laboratory in the city of Wuerzburg, Germany, Professor Wilhelm Röntgen was working with cathode rays and their properties when passing through glass when he discovered something unusual. Crystals on his desk near his current experiment suddenly started to glow. While he was not experimenting with fluorescence, he became curious about what was emerging in front of him. He tried to cover his tube with some heavy cardboard, yet the rays seemed to be still able to pass through. Röntgen got a wild idea and tested it to see if it could pass through human flesh (being a man of his time, he did not use his own hand – instead, he experimented on his wife's hand). And with that, one of the most significant discoveries in medical science was made. It was not because anyone was looking for it but because it had emerged out of curiosity. It had emerged because Röntgen allowed himself to look at a pattern he did not expect instead of immediately discarding it.

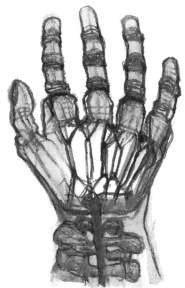

Some years later, Scottish physician Alexander Flemming returned from a holiday to discover mold on a discarded petri dish had prevented bacteria around it from growing. Not knowing what this was or why it had happened, Flemming followed his curiosity and started to explore the mold with his students. Thus, another invention saw the light of day as penicillin and took its rightful place in our medical toolbox.

Emerging discoveries with large potential happen at unpredictable times, in unexpected places. A team of scientists collecting sludge from a plastic bottle recycling plant in Japan led to the discovery of a plastic-eating bacteria. When European scientists tried to understand the bacteria, they accidentally made it hungry for PET plastic[33] used in single-use plastic bottles.

In the complex space, magic happens all around you.

UNPREDICTABLE THINGS EMERGE LIKE MAGIC RABBITS HOPPING AROUND YOU. IF YOU MANAGE TO CATCH ONE AND BRING IT BACK TO REALITY, WONDERFUL THINGS CAN HAPPEN.

Curiosity was what created penicillin. Had Flemming not been curious, penicillin would still have emerged but would have remained in the imaginary world, to no benefit to us living in the real world. X-rays would still exist even if Röngten hadn't discovered them. Only, no one would be able to use them in the real world. Who knows what other treasures are out there, waiting for someone to discover them? Maybe the cure for cancer is hopping around in a green field somewhere, but we are too busy or too constrained to catch it.

CURIOSITY IS THE ABILITY TO SPOT AND CATCH IDEAS, INVENTIONS, CONCEPTS, AND NOVELTIES IN THE IMAGINARY WORLD AND BRING THEM INTO REALITY.

The curiosity-driven innovation approach[34] is complimentary, not a replacement, to the more classic process of looking for a specific answer to a particular problem.

One of the great innovators, Thomas Edison, said in a 1929 press conference: *"None of my inventions came by accident. I see a worthwhile need to be met, and I make trial after trial until it comes."* Edison found a problem and insisted on solving that specific problem through experimentation and a lot of persistence. Having over a thousand patents to his name, it would seem that identifying a problem and looking for a viable solution works.

The thing to be aware of is that humans tend to stop searching when they have found what they are looking for. For many generations, this behavior made sense. The clan needs food, and the hunters go hunting, returning after harvesting enough game to feed the clan. Searching stopped when something plausible was achieved, notwithstanding what was possible. This was the proper priority; because why waste energy on better or more meat when you had harvested what could feed the clan?

While this approach worked for our predecessors searching for food, the first answer might not be the best regarding modern-day innovation.

Or even worse – the answer we are looking for, thinking it will be the best, makes us blind to other solutions.

When I look down at my shirt, it seems evident that buttons and buttonholes are two pieces of the same idea. Together they keep my shirt closed. Yet the magic rabbit "buttonhole" was caught 2300 years after the button was invented. Until then, buttons were decorative, and clothes were held together by other means. Cans existed for more than a century before the can opener. For a hundred years, people pried the can of food open with whatever piece of metal they had handy. In retrospect, it seems obvious, but apparently, the solution, albeit obvious, was overseen.

Most of us know the old experiment where you are asked to count the number of times a basketball is passed between players in a short movie clip[35]. During the clip, a man dressed as a gorilla walks between the players, doing a little dance. As the participants are so focused on counting the number of basketball passes, most miss the gorilla.

This experiment was taken a step further in a 2013 study[36]. A group of radiologists was given the familiar task of studying CT images and looking for lung nodules. A picture of a gorilla, 48 times larger than the lung nodules, was inserted in the last case. Eye tracking technology revealed that the radiologists were, at some point, looking directly at the location of the gorilla. You would think that radiologists trained to spot small anomalies in a CT scan would detect a picture of a gorilla, orders of magnitude larger than what they were looking for, yet 83% of them missed the gorilla. So, even experts operating within their domain of expertise are vulnerable to inattentional blindness.

WE MIGHT MISS ALL THE MAGIC RABBITS RUNNING AROUND US WHILE WE HUNT FOR A HARE.

Magicians use this property as well. In the introduction to the book, when explaining close-up magic we briefly touched on the concept of "misdirection". Inattentional blindness is the science behind misdirection and why close-up magicians encourage spectators to pay close attention. It makes the magic trick seem even more fair and impossible when the magician tells the spectator to look closely for any sneaky business.

What the magician is doing is creating the space for inattentional blindness.

If the spectator is convinced that the coin is still in the right hand, calling attention to that hand will allow for the left hand to use the spectator's "blindness" to do what needs to be done without being detected.

A trick I often did as a close-up magician is a classic called "card under drink," and it might be a good example to explain inattentional blindness. This was the trick that taught me how to utilize this concept to achieve an effect that reads as impossible on paper, yet most close-up magicians will be happy to show it to you, should you encounter one.

I have a card selected and signed with a pen by a spectator, removing any chance of me using an extra card. I shuffle the card into the deck and tell the spectator that the card will appear under my drink – usually a can of soda or whatever beverage the establishment has available.

I attempt to find the card like a normal magic trick, but when I apparently find the wrong one, I say: *"Oh wait – that's because the card is under the drink."* I point to the drink, and underneath – like a coaster – is a card – the selected, signed card. Usually, tricks are never to be repeated, but this particular trick is a lot of fun to repeat. First, the card appears under the drink a couple of times while I encourage the spectator to look closely and try to catch me. As a finale, the entire deck of cards is under the drink while I hold the selected card in my hand.

Doing this trick for many years taught me the inner workings of this blindness. The word "misdirection" might be a misnomer, as it is more "direction." As I point at the drink, saying: *"Watch closely, the card will end up under the drink,"* the hand that is not pointing is palming the card. "Palming" is a method magicians use to secretly dislodge a card from the deck and conceal it in the palm. As I say: "*... and please shuffle the cards,*" I pass the deck of cards to the spectator while moving the drink out of the way. During that action, I secretly deposit the card under the drink from the palm. The attention is on the deck, as the spectator still thinks the card is somewhere in the shuffled deck. To achieve this, I am utilizing something called gaze-following[37].

As humans, we are hard-wired to follow the gaze of someone looking intently at something. Our ancestors living on the savanna found that when someone is looking intently at something, it might be a danger or it might be food, and those who followed the gaze survived. So, looking where someone else is looking is in our DNA. By the way, if you are a leader, eye gazing helps promote psychological safety if you make sure to look at those who might otherwise be left out. Other group members listen to that person more, and group performance increases. Eye gazing also increases people's willingness to contribute to group discussions[38].

There's an old story about a man looking for his car keys. He is searching for the keys under the streetlight and not in the alley where he lost them because the lighting is better here. This has given name to "the streetlight effect", in which we tend to look for solutions in the areas where we have the best data. This leads to sub-optimal solutions 50% of the time[39].

While misdirection's psychological and cognitive science is well established, the neuroscientific explanations are incomplete. It is still an unsolved problem. The problem is sometimes associated with The Binding Problem[40] and is the theory of how objects and emotions processed by different parts of the brain are bound together into a single experience. The brain is a neural system that evolved to run a physical body in a social environment and is subject to all manner of illusions[41].

Whether you work with the philosophy of mind, cognitive science, or neuroscience, the approaches vary, and research is still ongoing[42]. Not so much whether misdirection works – we know it does because magicians have used it for hundreds of years. But we don't know exactly how a magician can control the spectator's focus to such a degree that a card can repeatedly be placed under a drink, clearly visible on the table, unseen to the spectator. Even the binding problem itself is being challenged as an ill-posed question.[43]

This is such a powerful tool that I can repeat the trick even when I explain to the spectators what is going on. In 1997 I first met one of the world's best performers of this trick. The resident magician at John Denver's bar in Aspen – Doc Eason. Working magic behind a bar meant that he had plenty of opportunities to do the trick, as a drink was always handy. When I told him I had a lot of fun with the trick and that I had spent a lot of time on the psychology behind it, he pulled out a deck of cards and continued to fool me, a seasoned magician, several times in a row, with the very same card under the drink.

When we focus, we focus. We don't have a concept of dynamic focus. If we had, the trick would no longer work because we would shift focus based on what matters, not what we are told matters.

As Charles H. Duell, commissioner of the US Patent office, never said in 1899: *"Everything that can be invented has been invented."* It's good that this quote is apocryphal because, as we have seen, the amount of magic rabbits in the imaginary world is infinite, and curiosity is the muscle you need to train to catch them. Unlike Pokémon, you do not have to catch them all.

There is a reason for painting this almost ridiculous image of unspotted opportunities as magic rabbits in an imaginary land. The more extreme a metaphor is, the better it will be remembered. This is why most memo techniques rely on radical and ridiculous pictures.

The idea of paying attention to things that "emerge" dates back to Aristotle[44], but just because we know about a theory does not mean we live by it. Most people recognize the idea about getting great ideas in the shower. Yet, the same people voluntarily install social media applications on their smartphones, ensuring their brain is fed entertainment continuously, even when it could have used a break to notice a rabbit carrying an awesome idea emerging right in front of them. Coincidentally, using a smartphone to fight boredom makes you more bored, not less[45]. When we are at rest – defined as free of input, our mind is allowed to wander, scientists found activities in multiple regions of the association cortex. They did not see a passive, silent brain during rest but rather a brain full of creativity[46].

Some companies have dedicated innovation teams, but enabling everybody to catch a rabbit might be better. To do that, they need more than just curiosity. Teams need dynamic focus.

So how do we enable employees to seamlessly work with both reality and imagination? It's a dynamic we will introduce in the next chapter.

BREAK ON THROUGH
(TO THE OTHER SIDE)

How
DYNAMIC FOCUS
will supercharge innovation

Take a look at the governing constraints in your organization. Are employees encouraged – or maybe even incentivized – to reach their goals quickly and efficiently while delivering good quality?

That is probably good if your organization's work is firmly grounded in reality, with established best practices. You do not need innovation, and factory workers at a conveyor belt will slow production down if they're not 100% focused on their goals and targets.

If you work with complex problems however, there is an opportunity here. If your organization's success relies on being innovative, you work in a complex environment, and then you need "Dynamic Focus."

Dynamic focus is the agency of the employees to pursue a magic rabbit should they spot one, without fear of repercussions because they stray away from a target set by a manager somewhere. Who knows, other animals might be waiting to be caught, such as **black swans**[47] or **dragon kings**[48].

For a long time, swans were believed to be all white, but it only took one observation of **Cygnus atratus** – the black swan – to change this perception. As human beings, we are very good at observing and measuring the world around us, leading to a rather dogmatic worldview. We often search for evidence for those beliefs we have already formed, to the extent that we ignore evidence that contradicts those beliefs. The black swan analogy is all about challenging what we think we know. No one was looking for black swans in particular, but when we accidentally observed one, it immediately changed our view of swans. When scientists found the carcass of a platypus, they couldn't bring themselves to believe it was a real animal[49]. After all, it had the tail of an otter, the beak of a duck, fur like a beaver, and it laid eggs. It wasn't until a live one was caught that it was finally believed to be a real animal.

We might also be lucky to catch a dragon king, which is a double metaphor in that a dragon king is rare or unique like a dragon and can have a significant impact or substantial size like a king. The difference between a dragon king and a black swan is that dragon kings could be observed had we expanded our field of interest to be big enough or dared to look for a dragon king where we otherwise would not go looking for data.

When looking at the financial crisis in 2008, economists can clearly explain why it happened by looking at data that was available back then. That makes it a dragon king event. The printing press is another example of a dragon king event because it revolutionized the production and dissemination of information in Europe and beyond. It enabled the mass printing of books, pamphlets, newspapers, and other documents that were previously copied by hand or by expensive and slow methods. It also facilitated the spread of ideas, knowledge, culture, religion, and political movements that shaped the modern world. The printing press was not a random or unpredictable invention; it was influenced by factors such as papermaking technology, metalworking skills, artistic creativity, and market demand. It also had some precursors and indicators that can be traced back to ancient China and Korea. Along the same lines, the internet and Artificial Intelligence could also be classified as dragon kings.

The next time you feel your innovation workshop isn't going as well as you had hoped, stand up and open a window. You never know, a black swan might fly in.

DYNAMIC FOCUS IS THE TRUST THAT THE EMPLOYEE IS COMPETENT ENOUGH TO DECIDE IF THE POTENTIAL VALUE OF CHASING THE OPPORTUNITY OUTWEIGHS THE VALUE OF THE CURRENT GOAL.

Remember that humans are hard-wired to do this by default. Some might be afraid that this empowerment will lead to people chasing rabbits all day long instead of producing value, but humanity has always lived and thrived like this.

Neurotransmitters regulate our brains. If the body wants to reward us, it releases dopamine. If a saber tooth tiger attacks and we need to fight, it releases epinephrine (adrenaline). Spending too much time thinking hard and increasing the cognitive load on your brain releases glutamate, and too much glutamate is believed to make us tired[50]. We literally get tired if we think too hard, just as we get tired if we work too hard. Humans are perfectly capable of balancing thinking and working. Otherwise, we wouldn't have survived as a species.

DYNAMIC FOCUS IS EMPOWERING EMPLOYEES TO SELF-GOVERN AND SELF-ORGANIZE IN A VIBRANT ENVIRONMENT, ALLOWING ONE OR MORE TEAM MEMBERS TO CHASE AN OPPORTUNITY.

Dynamic focus cannot rely on permission from a leader because the rabbit will be long gone by then.

One of the enablers of dynamic focus is serenity. Have you ever wondered why the best ideas come to us in the shower or during a long walk in the woods? The mental and relaxing downtime allows our brains to make connections we might not have made otherwise. We need the serenity to discover the rabbits. They will slip by our attention if we are too stressed or preoccupied. As a meta-reflection, this means that if you tend to pick up your phone every time you feel "micro-bored", you are countering serenity and, in turn, your ability to discover emergent ideas.

We already know how to work with dynamic focus. Look at kids playing in the playground. If they play soccer, they know the governing constraints, and all know how to follow the rules. Often, kids are playing "free play" where the rules – or absence of rules – are entirely dynamic. As long as the fun is maintained, anyone can suggest something new, and the group will follow, provided they feel a sense of belonging and it is fun and playful.

In the Danish language, this behavior is specific. The word for playing (as in sport) is quite different from that for playing (as kids do on a playground). The words are **"spil"** and **"leg."** This is the "leg" that forms the first half of the LEGO company name. The word LEGO is a combination of the words playing and well. **LEg GOdt -> LEGO.**

I believe that the success of the LEGO Group is firmly linked to their core idea that children are their role models. As Wittgenstein said[51]: *"The limits of my language mean the limits of my world."* Having grown up with a discourse that clearly separates playing within a ruleset (play) and free playing (leg), the Danes are particularly good at dynamic focus, and I assume that the LEGO Group was destined to be a Danish company, even when it was an undiscovered magic rabbit waiting for someone to catch it.

The connection between agency and children is not new. Without going too much into academics, a few honorable mentions are in place. The Swiss philosopher Jean Piaget was building on the autonomy described by Immanuel Kant and Friedrich Nietzsche but in the context of social interaction between children[52]. The American psychologist Lawrence Kohlberg extended Piaget's research and included Kant and Nietzche's theories that the governing body was morality. He breaks down morals into different levels and uses that to explain why sometimes children who are otherwise playing well can end up fighting if an external element with a different level of morals enters the group.

Those of us who have kids know how this plays out. Children are free-playing (leg), making up the rules on the fly. *"Hey, let's pretend the treehouse is a spaceship."* *"Oh, let's say that the grass is lava."* The imagination quickly reacts to these new inputs and continues effortlessly playing. That is until a new kid with a different "moral" enters the group, and the free play comes to a grinding halt. The kids will then have to resort to playing ("spil") something with a ruleset or cease playing altogether. Until then, the kids self-organize, allowing some – or all – to chase whatever idea emerges from their collected imagination.

DYNAMIC FOCUS CANNOT RELY ON PERMISSION FROM A LEADER BECAUSE THE RABBIT WILL BE LONG GONE BY THEN.

Of course, a professional team working in an organization differs from children playing on a playground. But now that we understand what dynamic focus is, how do we enable it in your organization? Enable it so that the result is a more innovative organization that still serves the need and reason for its existence.

We have argued that agency is self-governed by "moral beings" doing the right thing and, therefore, cannot be permission-based. The role of the leader who wants to create dynamic focus is to create the space for it. That is a space of trust and faith in the people.

To create the space for employees to **be** something is to create the space for them to **have** something. The ability to **be** something based on something you **have** is the etymological basis of the word **behavior.**

For you to **be** brave, you need to **have** courage. You need to **have** humor to **be** funny. You cannot **be** clever without **having** intellect. The space you need to create for your employees is the ability to **have**, because without **have** there is no **be**.

This is a complex problem, and as such, there is no best practice you can follow. I can offer some inspiration, namely how we created The Leadership Playground at the LEGO Group.

COME TO-GETHER

How the
INNOVATIVE
LEADERSHIP MODEL
that powers the LEGO Group came to be

I was fortunate enough to participate in creating the global leadership model for the LEGO Group. I will describe the process we went through below, and as you will see, the model resembles the above theory. Before I continue, it is important to say that the theoretical framework discussed above is mine. The leadership model you will see below is a group effort, and while I brought my theories forward, they were not simply adapted but treated as any other input. While The Leadership Playground is compatible with my thoughts, it is not my model. It was a group effort, and my role was no more prominent or important than anyone else's in the group.

Creating a new leadership model is complex – it makes little sense to copy what someone else has done because the many moving parts of an organization mean that copying a model is as right as it is wrong. The new model had to be created **by** the LEGO Group **for** the LEGO Group. The facilitation was chosen to be done by the International Institute for Management and Development – IMD. A prestigious private business school in Lausanne, Switzerland.

In May 2018, we all met up in the Swiss Alps to kick off the work. The CEO and the CPO empowered the group to answer three questions:

1. SHOULD WE REPURPOSE OUR CURRENT THINKING ON LEADERSHIP AND/OR DEVISE A NEW LEADERSHIP MODEL?

2. IF YES, WHAT SHOULD THE LEADERSHIP MODEL LOOK LIKE?

3. WHAT IS THE MOST EFFECTIVE IMPLEMENTATION APPROACH?

Notice how the first two questions are perfectly shaped to be answered in the unconstrained imaginary world. They clarified that we were empowered to create something inspirational rather than directional. Only at step 3 would we need to bring the solution to reality.

The delicate choice of words used to empower is noteworthy. They used pictures and feelings in the wordings, such as *"Create something that can be used as a mirror – something anyone can hold up at the end of a meeting and ask if we have lived up to these principles."* The group's joint feeling of responsibility was significant, and we all felt the agency, empowerment, and commitment to create something wonderful.

The first thing we did was to diverge by exploring widely, without any concern about whether it was possible. We interviewed many of our colleagues, leaders, and specialists, getting raw, qualitative data points.

We also analyzed our existing leadership models and found more than 100 artifacts from 25 different models and frameworks. The LEGO Group is a large organization; we have had several leadership models over the years. Even those decommissioned still lived in pockets, and their artifacts were still in use. Seeing how complex we had made leadership in our efforts to simplify it with tools and methodologies was an eye-opener.

To begin the convergence to reality, we made some decisions.

WE WOULD SCRAP ALL THE EXISTING MODELS – at least as mandatory. If someone found them helpful, they would be free to use the models, but it was no longer institutionalized.

WE WANTED TO CREATE SOMETHING THAT WOULD LAST. Something that would be just as relevant in times of headwind as in times of tailwind.

WE WANTED TO CREATE SOMETHING UNIQUE TO THE LEGO GROUP so that anyone who saw the model would immediately recognize the LEGO Group's spirit.

LEADERSHIP IS AN ACT, NOT A POSITION. Anyone can take leadership upon themselves, and it is not based on a title. The model we wanted to create should speak to every employee.

CHILDREN ARE OUR ROLE MODELS – we do not want to create a leadership model but a leadership playground. A playground provides a safe space with some guardrails to encourage free play.

These were still hypotheses, so we re-interviewed the colleagues we had interviewed before, asking for early feedback on our principles. We collected all the data on giant post-its, covering several rooms at the Lausanne campus, and started workshopping on the data.

We had some challenging discussions at this point because there were so much data and so much input that we wanted to include while still keeping the model simple. We turned to our hosts and facilitators – the professors and staff that IMD had assigned to help us.

IMD facilitated a decision workshop, where we decided that our model would focus on what the LEGO Group needed. While that sounds like a straightforward statement, it helped us to move forward. We could remove "quality" from the model because Quality is already part of our Brand Framework, and the LEGO Group is already world-renowned for creating quality products.

Just because a word wasn't going to be in the model didn't mean the word wasn't important.

We now felt better converging.

The space we wanted to create ended up being the following:

BRAVE – CURIOUS – FOCUSED

We long debated how different cultures understand and comprehend the chosen words. Given that we had a lot of representation in the group, it was a great debate. I remember thinking that I had been in way too many meetings talking about how different cultures, races, or genders would react to something without having those present in the meeting. This made me appreciate the diversity of the working group even more, as we quickly covered a lot of ground.

We discussed if "Brave" was the right word for a while because we, to some extent, wanted the opposite. To create the space for everyone to speak their mind, even if they weren't brave. Nor should you have to be brave to speak up – it should be natural. In the end, we decided that our colleagues were smart enough to understand what the model was conveying, and we liked the simplicity of the word.

"Curious" was the space we least debated, as it resonated immediately, while "focused" probably was the one we pivoted on the most. We wanted to enable the employees to focus, creating what is truly valuable, but focus means many different things depending on what area you are working in. We decided to keep it and let it mean what people wanted it to mean. The LEGO Group is a diverse workplace with different types of work being done, and we wanted a model that could resonate both with the blue-collar workers in the factories and the marketeers in marketing. It was built into the model that it was not directive – it had to be interpreted.

We created a short manifesto:

WE'RE PLEASED TO INTRODUCE YOU TO YOUR LEADERSHIP PLAYGROUND DEVELOPED ENTIRELY BY AND FOR THE LEGO GROUP. THE LEADERSHIP PLAYGROUND IS A SPACE WHERE:

- Leadership is an act, not a position. The responsibility of leadership at the LEGO Group belongs to everyone at the LEGO Group

- Leadership is expressed by individuals in the actions and words they choose and not prescribed in a "one-size-fits-all" cookbook

- Leadership is demonstrated by everyone in the common things that we all do and not in grand gestures alone

- Leadership should bring even greater joy to our consumers and shoppers

- Leadership should energize everybody every day

ENERGIZE: Through being brave, more focused and staying curious.

EVERYBODY: Diversity and individuality. Everyone has a leadership responsibility for the LEGO Group.

EVERY DAY: Observable everyday actions that make a difference in your daily work.

The feedback was overwhelming and positive. We had reduced hundreds of artifacts into three simple spaces. Create the space for us to be brave, curious, and focused. We had effectively introduced self-organization and leadership as an act in one sentence. I remember saying: *"My fear is, this will make good leaders better, but bad leaders worse."* I was afraid that some leaders were relying on their ability to follow directions, use templates, and just by being structured, they could hold a leadership position. We were now requiring leaders to understand what they were doing. Even if that understanding was individual, leadership was no longer transactional.

As for implementing the model, we decided to create a movement instead of a cascade.

We had noticed that all the previous leadership models had been cascaded down into the organization from the top. Maybe we would have better luck letting this grow organically by creating a movement, finding people who immediately fell in love with the model, and asking them to be playground builders. Playground builders are employees who love the model and help build the playground locally, understanding and appreciating the differences in culture, work, and people.

At the time of writing, The Leadership Playground model is still the only one in the LEGO Group and continuously shows value. The LEGO Group measures the motivation of the employees often, and the results place the company at the absolute best in class when it comes to happy and motivated employees.

If you are curious about the finer details, IMD has published a case study including all the above information and much more, available from IMD.com, and there are more details on the model itself on LEGO.com. There is much more to the story than presented here, but I hope this was enough to give you ideas and inspiration.

In 2023 the LEGO Group together with IMD was awarded a Gold Reward from EFMD Global (European Foundation for Management Development) in the category of Organizational Development for The Leadership Playground[2].

The model turned out to be an excellent vehicle for motivation. In the next chapter, let's explore the mysteries and differences between motivation and satisfaction.

---

[2] You can read more about it at efmdglobal.org.

(I CAN'T GET NO) SATIS-FACTION

Why it is a fallacy to think
a leader or a magician can motivate anyone

AND WHAT
TO DO INSTEAD

I was standing on a stage in my dark outfit. I was fully aware of the hundreds of people sitting there, looking at me, listening to my every word. The lighting was intense, and I was squinting.

After being in lockdown due to the Corona pandemic, it was great to be back in my black suit. I don't usually wear suits, but I aim for a consistent look when in front of a big audience.

My purpose today on the stage was to inspire the audience to think, feel, or do something they otherwise wouldn't have thought, felt, or done.

My purpose was to fill them with wonder. To inspire them to do things they never thought they would or even could do on their own.

Time slowed down.
For the briefest moment,
I thought:
**"AM I HERE ON STAGE AS
A MAGICIAN OR A SENIOR
EXECUTIVE?"**

The magician and the leader were there to motivate the audience to do, think, or feel something that they otherwise wouldn't have done, thought, or felt had I not been there. There would be no reason for me to stand there if they could.

The leader and the magician's livelihoods depend on satisfaction; Satisfied spectators for the magician and satisfied employees for the leader. As a leader, you also have the added bonus of customer/user satisfaction. Whether you are a hospital leader or create innovative digital products, you depend on satisfied end users.

THIS CHAPTER IS ABOUT THE MOST IMPORTANT PEOPLE FOR THE LEADER: THE EMPLOYEES.

Employee satisfaction has always been a cornerstone of my leadership. I believe that employee satisfaction is a leading indicator of company success.

It makes me proud that for the past 15 years, my employee satisfaction score on a scale from 1-100 has never been below 80, and I had years where it was above 90.

High employee satisfaction does not necessarily make me a good leader, and I am not strutting these numbers to brag. My peers often challenge me that it signals someone who is not pushing the employees hard enough and is a sign of laissez-faire leadership. Your mileage may vary.

If you as a manager need to push your employees to perform, then the motivation to act may be unclear to the employee.

Pushing might cause stress. I do not claim to have the ultimate answer, and this chapter will only be valuable if you buy into the premise that employee satisfaction positively impacts business performance.

When I started doing magic, I would practice all the time. While watching TV, I would have a deck of cards in my hands, doing various sleights. When driving a car, I would have a coin palmed in my hand to enhance my palming capabilities. I would always have a deck of cards in my pocket when attending social events, ready to share some delightful tricks if asked.

I was an amateur. In the purest sense of the word: Someone who does something because they love to do it.

Some people love to nurture their gardens. They can spend hours in their garden, removing weeds and growing plants. They are amateurs.

Some love to play an instrument. They pick up the guitar or sit by the piano and create wonderful music, delighting those around them.

AMATEURS

Sometime in the 20th century, amateur started to mean something else. It started to represent someone of less skill than the professionals, those who got paid. After all, if you were good enough to get paid, why wouldn't you?

What drives a person to practice the guitar every day without getting paid? What makes a person spend hours in the garden, or painting beautiful paintings, without getting paid?

WHAT IS THE SECRET OF THE AMATEUR?

There have been many, more or less similar, studies with kids who get rewarded for doing something they love. Two groups of kids are playing in separate rooms, building towers. One of the groups starts to get incentivized to complete the towers. At some point, the incentives stop. The group that had earned rewards for completing the tower stopped playing. The other group continued to play, still finding it fun[53]. Does that mean there is a dichotomy? We can either love what we do or get paid for what we do, but not both? Fortunately, no – let's explore this fascinating topic.

The power of the amateur is fragile, yet most companies find themselves in a vicious circle when it comes to motivating their employees. They inadvertently sap the enjoyment of work by imposing bureaucratic measures, regulatory constraints, and excessive oversight. As a misguided attempt to boost employee motivation, they may implement performance management programs, incentive structures, and bonus schemes, often exacerbating the situation.

HIRE AMATEURS, AND TREAT THEM PROFESSIONALLY RATHER THAN HIRE PROFESSIONALS AND TREAT THEM AMATEURISHLY.

The key point to understanding motivation is that you cannot motivate anyone.

YOU CAN INCENTIVIZE PEOPLE TO DO SOMETHING, BUT MOTIVATION IS THE INTERNAL DRIVE OF THE AMATEUR.

You cannot force or buy motivation any more than you can force or buy love. Sure, you can buy something that looks like it, but it isn't real.

What you can do is create the space for the employee's motivation to grow. The book "Drive: The Surprising Truth About What Motivates Us[54]" introduces agency as a key component. Agency is the sense of control and autonomy individuals feel over their lives and work. When individuals have a high sense of agency, they feel they have the power to make choices and direct their own lives, leading to greater motivation and engagement. The book argues that traditional external motivators, such as rewards and punishments, can undermine agency and intrinsic motivation because they communicate to individuals that their behavior is controlled by external forces rather than by their own choices and values. Instead, it advocates for a model of motivation that focuses on fostering intrinsic motivation and agency through the promotion of autonomy, mastery, and purpose.

This agency is one of the things *dynamic focus* achieves. While we argued that the primary output of dynamic focus is increased innovation, we can similarly argue that the primary outcome is motivated employees.

There is an awareness point here, though.

IT'S A COMMON MISCONCEPTION THAT LEADERS CAN DIRECTLY MOTIVATE PEOPLE.

The reality is that motivation comes from within an individual, and a leader's role is to create an environment that fosters and supports that intrinsic motivation.

While leaders can't directly control or manipulate an individual's motivation, they can influence it through their actions and the environment they create. A leader can create the space necessary for individuals to feel engaged and motivated in their work.

They can create a positive and supportive culture that values and recognizes the contributions of team members. They can also help individuals connect their work to a larger purpose or mission that is meaningful to them. That means that while motivating someone is a meta-activity, demotivating people is a real thing.

What demotivates people differs from person to person, but here is a bullet list to illustrate what you as a leader can stop doing tomorrow that will lead to more motivated employees.

COMMON DEMOTIVATORS:

- Micromanaging: Leaders who micromanage their employees can create a sense of frustration and a lack of trust among their team members.

- Lack of recognition: Employees who feel their hard work and contributions are not recognized or appreciated can quickly become demotivated.

- Unclear expectations: Leaders who fail to provide clear expectations can leave their team members feeling insecure and demotivated.

- Lack of opportunities for growth: Employees who feel like there are no opportunities for growth, learning, or advancement within their organization can quickly become demotivated.

"THERE IS A MYTH ABOUT THAT THERE IS SUCH A THING AS 'MOTIVATION'. THERE IS NO SUCH THING AS MOTIVATION."

BAZ LUHRMANN

Motivation is not a thing. It is an internal desire to move. You can clear the path or get in the way, but the movement comes from the individual. As Newton's first law states: An object in motion stays in motion. When we are motivated, we can create a virtuous cycle of self-motivation because we are moving in a direction that feels right for us. This also means that getting started is immensely difficult if we are halted in this movement. Do not demotivate your employees. Be aware of the space you create, and be aware of the space the employee needs.

Let's take a closer look at how magic can help us identify this mystical space. It will require us to take a few steps up to the next platform.

STAIR-WAY TO HEAVEN

Opening the door to the quintessential space where
MAGIC LIVES

M agic is often described as "smoke and mirrors, sleight of hand."
But magic is not created with mirrors, trap doors, or sleight of
hand. It is created in the space between people. Sometimes between the
performer and the spectator, but more often between the spectators.

While the magician might set off a sequence of events through actions and words, the waves of thoughts, feelings, and emotions are those of the spectators. These waves can cause interference and resonance and build up to something much more than they were when initiated. Just as gently pushing a swing can cause it to swing higher and higher, magicians know how to work the aether between the audiences to increase their effects. Like a stairway, we move the feeling of experiencing something magic gently level by level.

To illustrate this, we will go on a bit of a detour. I will try to explain the most straightforward trick I do (from a sleight-of-hand perspective), which in turn is quite elaborate from a sleight-of-mouth perspective, as it is an effect within the effect, taking place entirely in the space between the spectators.

After having done an effect – as we magicians call it – where I demonstrate how verbal manipulation works, I take a spoon from my inner pocket. I want to make sure the audience sees that I'm holding a spoon, so I tell an irrelevant story about how mirror images behave when looking at the head of a spoon. I ask if anyone knows what happens with the mirror image if you look at the concave side of the spoon. And is it the same looking at the convex side? The mirror image is upside down when looking at the convex side of a well-polished spoon head. Will the image still be upside down if I rotate the spoon upside down while still looking at the convex side? I demonstrate this by rotating the spoon and looking into my own mirror image. Then I say:

"This is not really an effect about convex mirrors. It is about the fact that you see with your ears."

"It is not until I say the word FORK that you notice that I have demonstrated all this with a fork, not a spoon."

As I say the word fork, I hold my hands still so everyone can clearly see a fork.

"As I used the word spoon repeatedly, your brain made you see a spoon. You were seeing with your ears."

"Now, some of you will swear you saw a spoon in the beginning, while others, who are not so easily deceived, will have seen a fork all along."

THIS IS WHERE THE MAGIC REALLY BEGINS.
THE NARRATIVE DRIVES THE EFFECT.

I know my audience well. I understand that some people hate to admit they were fooled by magic, even the ones trying to hide it. So, when I say, *"Others, not so easily deceived, will have seen a fork all along,"* I trigger something in these people. Regardless of whether they paid attention, they will swear they always saw a fork, and there never was a spoon. My words did not fool them!

They still think the effect they witnessed was that my words were enough to cause some to see a spoon by merely talking about it.

They think that my words fooled those who saw a spoon, and they don't want to admit that such shenanigans fooled them.

They will insist that they saw a fork all along, making the people who are sure they saw a spoon scratch their head.

Now, this radically reinforces the effect among the (majority) of the spectators who could swear they saw a spoon and indeed were "seeing with their ears."

Please don't tell anyone. I did indeed cheat and used sleight of hand to switch a spoon for a fork. There really was a spoon at the beginning, and it had nothing to do with verbal manipulation. At least not the kind I led them to believe they were witnessing.

It is a trick within a trick.

There's the trick they think they witnessed and then the trick they actually experienced.

I love to see the "waves" of debate in the audience. It usually starts in the back. The people who dislike being fooled by magic often position themselves in the back. They will loudly claim that they saw a fork all along and openly debate those who admit they saw a spoon.

The magic happens in the narrative – it appears in the relationship between the audience as they talk about their different experiences. It exists only in the aether between the people.

Had I shown this to just one person, the effect would be that there was a spoon first, and then – by magic – I was holding a fork. It would be a neat trick but not a memorable experience.

THE REAL MAGIC HAPPENS WHEN A CROWD SEES THE SAME THING BUT EXPERIENCES SOMETHING DIFFERENT.

The effect arises when they talk about what they witnessed, causing the cognitive waves to interfere.

By introducing the aether as a secret element and allowing the trick to live in that element, it grows to something much bigger. Even after I leave the establishment, the effect continues to exist and grow as more people share what they have experienced.

This is the real illusion of magic, and the idea of a narrative existing in the space between people is something we can learn from. While it is a powerful concept in magic, it is even more potent in the world of leadership and people.

The power of narratives is one of the most substantial transformational learning pieces discussed in this book.

It all begins with a rather ridiculous claim: You are not you.

NO-THING COMPARES 2 U

YOU ARE NOT YOU

In many different organizational contexts,
you are your narrative.

"She was nothing like I had expected!" We often hear that sentence when people meet someone for the first time whom they have only heard stories about up until that meeting.

STORIES CAN STRONGARM FACTS.

They move faster and are easier to remember. Ask anyone how our taste buds work. The prevailing belief regarding the human tongue is that it possesses distinct regions dedicated to each of the primary tastes: sour, sweet, salty, and bitter. This notion, often illustrated through the well-known "tongue map," perpetuates the idea that our taste buds are neatly compartmentalized, each serving a specific purpose in our gustatory experience.

The only problem is that this is not factual[55]. It is an easy-to-remember story. Taste buds are, in fact, capable of detecting all tastes, irrespective of their location on the tongue. The reality is that our taste buds function far more complexly, each containing taste receptor cells that can simultaneously identify multiple taste qualities.

Despite the evidence refuting the tongue map's accuracy, this misconception persists in the public consciousness due to the power of narratives and stories. People are often more likely to remember and share information presented in a captivating story, regardless of its factual veracity. The tongue map offers a simple, appealing narrative that is easily understood and disseminated, contributing to its enduring presence in popular culture. This phenomenon highlights the strength of stories in shaping our understanding of the world, demonstrating that they can sometimes hold more sway than empirical facts.

Most of those who have been teaching or giving lectures have heard about learning styles – that some people are auditory learners, tactile learners, visual learners etc. and this myth is still found in many schools and teaching materials. Even though it has been repeatedly proven not to be true[56] and even, to some extent, counters learning,[57] it is widely taught because it is a good story that you can relate to. Myths live longer if a story backs them.

Your narrative is the dominating story that the organization is telling about you. And it is more consistent than you think – or you might like.

Your narrative is the stories people in the organization tell about you. *"Do you know Alex from finance? We're meeting next week."* A common question that is asked, in various shapes and forms, many times; Sometimes, it is innocent, like in the above example. Sometimes, it is just gossip. Everything that is said about you shapes your narrative.

People get promoted due to their narrative. Some even get fired if they have a particularly bad narrative. One might try to change the dominant story with different behavior, but changing an established, dominating story in an organization is quite tricky. Even if a person changes and the narrative doesn't, consequences (good or bad) might still happen. You are not you in an organization. You are your narrative, and you might not even know if your narrative is good or bad[58].

NAPOLEON WAS SHORT. EVERYONE KNOWS THAT. OR AT LEAST, THAT'S WHAT PEOPLE ARE SAYING. HE WAS CALLED "LE PETIT CAPORAL" AS A SIGN OF AFFECTION, BUT "PETITE," MEANING "SMALL," SUGGESTED THAT PEOPLE THOUGHT HE WAS SMALL UP UNTIL THEY MET HIM AND SAW THAT HE WAS OF AVERAGE HEIGHT. THE STORY OF HIM BEING SMALL WAS MORE DOMINANT THAN THE ACTUAL FACT.

Stories have been the vehicle used to share and maintain what we know about a person for thousands of years. If you are important enough, your story might be written down, but for most of us, our stories live amongst those who tell them.

Specifically, we are talking about the stories told about us in an organizational context.

When you look at the stars at night, you might recognize a given star constellation. The first one I learned to identify was The Great Bear. At some point, someone placed meaning on those stars. That's why we, among millions of stars, recognize them. There have probably been many interpretations over the years, and this became the dominating story at some point. And once it became the dominating story, it stuck. This is probably why America is not called Columbia, but is named after an Italian explorer named Amerigo by a German mapmaker who, in 1507, made a map and thought "America" sounded cooler. His naming became the dominant story, and the names on previous maps didn't stick.

If we see this as a metaphor for your organizational narrative, who created yours? Someone was characterizing you. Somehow, down the road, your story was shaped into what it is today.

Just as the magician carefully constructs and orchestrates the narrative around a given effect, **you can direct your own narrative**. You can influence what is being said and how the story is told.

How long does a narrative live? A story can only survive by being told and retold. There are a few interesting scientific articles regarding the longevity of stories and how long they live once "in the aether."

The study *"Comparative phylogenetic analyses uncover the ancient roots of Indo-European folktales[59]"* use something called Phylogenetics which is primarily used by biologists as it is the study of evolutionary relationships among biological entities. By applying autologistic actor attribute models known from the world of statistics, scientists could trace back popular folk tales to their ancestral origin. **There is evidence that stories can live for thousands of years, and even signs of correlation between our words and our genes**[60]. While stories change a bit by being re-told, they preserve the emotional elements they contain, even when the inevitable changes to the original are happening[61].

Anthropologists, ethnologists, and linguists have long puzzled over why complex mythical stories appearing in cultures widely separated in space and time are similar. The story of the star constellation "Great Bear" (Ursa Major) follows the same basic structure called "the cosmic hunt." The story spread in Africa, Europe, Asia, and the Americas 15,000 years ago, following the same basic storyline. The story of Pygmalion, a man who creates a beautiful sculpture and falls in love with it, is found in Greek mythology and among the Bara people of Madagascar[62]. It can be traced back to the Berbers 4,000 years ago when it was a figure carved out of a tree trunk instead of a sculpture. Phylogenetic reconstructions of stories show that stories transcend space and time. They live in the "aether" among people, surviving generations and passing through cultures and races.

Stories in this context are not, as Carl Jung claims, an artifact of a collective unconsciousness[63]. People create them, tell them, and they live in the aether between people. A story such as the cosmic hunt can survive 15,000 years, living entirely in the "aether." Stories survive by being told and endure only by being a captivating story worthy of being re-told.

The stories told most often become dominating stories.

A STORY CAN BECOME DOMINANT EITHER BY FREQUENCY, MAGNITUDE, OR BOTH.

A story that is told often and by many people is the most powerful.

Your story is precious. Once it is in "the aether," it has a life of its own. Catching and containing it is as tricky as catching smoke with a butterfly net. In the next chapter, we will discuss how you become the author of your own story.

The story told about you is you to anyone but yourself. Other people engage with you based on the story they believe is yours.

Understanding how personal narratives originate is essential and immensely powerful.

Stories live in the imaginary world. They are illusions of reality.

They can change into anything as they are told in the imaginary world. There are no limits.

WHO ARE YOU

The story of

HOW YOU ARE COMPOSED OF THE STORIES TOLD ABOUT YOU

I started scientific research in this area many years ago – more precisely, in 2012 when I was working on my second Master's degree. I continued the action learning and action research process for more than a decade after, collecting valuable data.

The idea that you are not you, but you are what the stories tell about you is not an entirely new scientific discovery. I stand on the shoulders of great thinkers in both philosophy and psychology.

Before we get to "you," let's start with "me" and "I." In 1934, the philosopher George Herbert Mead was interested in the self, and in particular, he did not subscribe to the theory prevalent at the time that we are a product of our genes[64]. Mead suggested instead that the "me" is a construct shaped through interaction with others. It is a cognitive object known only through retrospection, whereas the "I" is the subject. The American psychologist Kenneth Gergen builds on this with the concepts of a "self" and an "identity."[65] The personal identity is a construct of who has the dialogue, what they are saying, and to whom they are saying it.[66] In his book "The Saturated Self"[67] there's an interesting paragraph in this context:

"One's words remain nonsense (mere sounds or markings) until supplemented by others' assent (or appropriate action). And this assent, too, remains dumb until another (or others) lend it a sense of meaning. Any action from the utterance of a single syllable to the movement of an index finger, becomes language when others grant it significance in a pattern of interchange; and even the most elegant prose can be reduced to nonsense if others do not grant it the right of meaning. In this way, meaning is born of interdependence. And because there is no self outside a system of meaning, it may be said that relations precede and are more fundamental than self. Without relationship there is no language with which to conceptualize the emotions, thoughts, or intentions of the self."

The narrative relationship with others shapes the identity. Therefore, representing your "self" depends on what you say and the words you use – the discourse. I will use the word "discourse" here and mention that it might be closer to "dispositif." "Dispositif" is a word used by Foucault, which means an array of discourses that implies a particular behavior without being deterministic. He uses an example of a prison – Jeremy Bentham's Panopticon – constructed with a guard tower in the middle with dimmed windows. The prisoners are unaware of whether they are observed or not and choose to behave exemplarily. We govern ourselves according to the discourse surrounding us.

Let's exemplify this: May is a new lawyer in the firm, and she is being introduced to the others by the boss, walking around the office: "Oh, and over here is John. He's the hardest worker of us all. You'll have to get up early if you want to get the results he's getting." says the boss. While this might flatter John, it also has an impact on him. He feels forced to show up early and go home late because of the story everyone is telling about him. While the discourse is not deterministic – it is not forcing John to stay late – it influences him. The discourse creates an expectation that he tries to live up to.

Psychologists Rosenthal and Jacobson conducted an interesting experiment.[68] A teacher was told that a given class consisted of talented and promising students. At the end-of-year test, the students performed much better than a control group composed of similar students. The mere expectation is enough to drive behavior. The effect is called "The Pygmalion Effect," named after Greek mythology. The story goes that the sculptor fell in love with a statue of a beautiful woman and so desired her to be real. She turned real due to the expectations, and they married. This story inspired the story of "My Fair Lady," where a poor flower girl becomes a fine lady. Although the initial results from the Rosenthal experiment have been disputed[69], the original hypothesis is sound, and several recent studies support it. In 2023, a study showed that getting diagnosed with a learning disability or other labels would influence the student's grade just by the label itself[70].

The opposite effect has also been tested and tried as well. Nicknamed "The Golem Effect," it shows that if a teacher expects poor performance, the students will perform poorly. It is in the same ballpark as placebo and nocebo

I hypothesize that the same effect is present in organizations. We have a narrative that we try to live up to. The narrative shapes us, and it shapes those around us. Your organizational narrative shapes other people's expectations of you. Your "me" rather than your "I." This means that you can do a lot – work harder, work differently, but your "you" doesn't change if your narrative does not change.

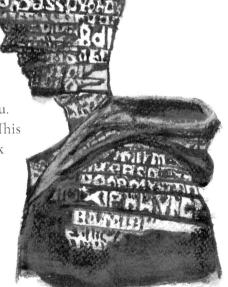

The English sociologist Anthony Giddens says, *"A person's identity is not to be found in behavior, nor – important though this is – in the reactions of others, but in the capacity to keep a particular narrative going."*[71]. He continues to describe how we cannot control this chain of quickly diverging events but can influence the source by either being the first to tell a new story or behaving in a way that will spawn a story. John Shotter follows this chain of thought and defines what he calls "conversational realities"[72] as the reality that is constructed by the narratives of others. He points out that you cannot simply make up a narrative, just like you can't just freely draw a star sign. It has to be based on existing stars. Similarly, your organizational narrative has to be based on existing behaviors experienced by several people.

To take control of your narrative is to take control of what you do and select the important "stars in the star signs." The stories you would like to be told. Stories survive by being told. They live in an "aether" composed of the relationship between people. That means stories can survive by being told and re-told by others through several layers of connections. However, as with all reflective and self-referencing processes, this poses a complication because a small mistake can quickly grow out of proportion. A small story can create dissonance or resonance and increase a part of your narrative if that particular story is told enough times. So not only do you have to figure out the stories to be told, but you also have to manage how they are being told.

Assuming you want to manage your narrative, what steps do you need to take? Let's look at an example:

Alex came stumbling into my office. *"It's going to open again. You know – the position!"* I instantly knew what "the position" meant. There was a role in the company that was considered a real career role. It involved a lot of responsibilities, but also a lot of travel and working at odd hours, so people only stayed in the role for a couple of years, but when they left, it was usually to a more senior role.

Alex wanted this role so badly and had applied for it the last time it was open but was told that the position was heavy on strategy, and they wanted someone more strategic.

Alex explained: *"I simply told them the truth the last time I interviewed for the role I have never done a strategy, so I don't know if I'm good at it. Who knows – maybe I am? I know the position will be available later this year. How can I get it this time?"*

"They are not hiring you for the role," I said, leaving a confused look on Alex's face. *"They are hiring the illusion of you – the story that is told about you. They hire your narrative."*

As you think about it, how many people know the real you? Maybe some of your closest friends or your significant other? But do your colleagues know the real you? Probably not. So it is only fair to assume that the hiring panel will not either. The best approximation of you they can come to know is to know your narrative.

Alex was not buying this entirely at this point. The confusion changed to resistance, and I remember telling Alex that I did not want to impose anything and offered to help in other ways than shaping the narrative. Alex explained that the hesitation was not because of disbelief but rather "not enough" belief. After I shared some of the theoretical background mentioned above, the concept began to make sense, and Alex wanted to move forward.

First, we defined the discourse. We agreed to focus on "strategist" rather than the word "strategy" because "strategist" is a person. At the next leadership meeting, an agenda point was "round the table" to introduce the leadership team to a newcomer who had just joined. Alex had practiced an "elevator pitch."

"As I think about it," said Alex, "I have improvised these introductions up until now, but they really are a perfect place to drop a potential piece of my narrative."

When it was Alex's turn to make an introduction, it was a well-rehearsed two minutes: "Well, I am first and foremost known as a strategist. I enjoy helping other teams and am often invited to help build strategies in various parts of the company. I'm not saying I'm an expert strategist – I think it's mainly because I don't mind lending a helping hand that people call me a strategist."

Alex was pleased with this first drop of deliberate storytelling. I had previously explained that people are cognitively lazy when it comes to others. So when someone asks "hey, do you know Alex?" the easiest thing to do is just to repeat the description that you just heard instead of making up your own description. But we had to make sure this was not just a "story told," but also a "story lived."

Soon after Alex had begun the new self-narrative, invitations started to drop in, requesting strategic help. Alex did a lot of pre-work, probably more than necessary, for the first few meetings to provide decent assistance to the team and not just selfishly improve a narrative.

The Pygmalion effect started to show its face, and as the expectations of Alex's expertise rose, Alex started living up to them. This led to some successful strategies, which people began to talk about at the water cooler.

My phone was buzzing, and I could see that it was Alex calling. I knew the interview was today, so I was curious to hear how it went.

"I hear you're quite the strategist!" Alex yelled. *"That was the opening remark from the recruiting manager!"* As expected, the narrative of Alex had preceded the actual meeting. More importantly, Alex had dramatically improved as a strategist, trying to live up to the expectations that such a narrative brings. The story that we created was not just a story. It brought some real transformation with it, as it helped Alex build the needed strategic capabilities.

The rest is, as they say, history. Alex got the job.

That was a condensed and anonymized example from the real world. The purpose was to bring some of the hairy theory into reality through an example that most people can relate to. The example demonstrated "stories lived" and "stories told" as well as the Pygmalion effect.

Sometimes, stories change based on a specific presentation. Hannibal Lecter is often remembered as a sophisticated and intelligent serial killer after Anthony Hopkins played him in the movie "Silence of the Lambs", but he was originally written as a much more brutal and animalistic character in Thomas Harris' novel "Red Dragon". Frankenstein's monster is remembered as a mute and nincompoop monster looking very much like how Boris Karloff portrayed the monster in the 1930s. In contrast, the monster in Mary Shelly's novel is quite sophisticated, speaks several languages, and looks nothing like how it is portrayed and remembered.

As the legendary song "As Time Goes By" popularized by the movie Casablanca might have said:

YOU MUST REMEMBER THIS

A narrative's just a story

That was told to you

And you're still telling it too

Chorus:

As time goes by

The facts get lost

And the narrative grows

As time goes by

It's easy to get lost

In the stories we compose

The past is just a tale

That we choose to believe

But sometimes it's hard to tell

What's really true and what we weave

ANOTHER BRICK IN THE WALL

Learn a complete

MAGIC ROUTINE YOU CAN USE TO ENHANCE YOUR PRESENTATIONS

When I do large presentations and would like an active audience who asks questions or come with comments, I find that doing a quick engagement with the audience warms them up.

If I bring my people together in a room, it is because I want their feedback. Otherwise, I might just have recorded a video. Live presentations, at least for me, are an invitation to dialogue.

The following is a trick I have used on those occasions. I will explain how the trick looks to the audience, and then I will teach you all the details needed to be able to perform this the next time you're doing a large presentation

Magic is 99% showmanship and 1% the secret. Sometimes, the showmanship is left to the reader, leaving just the secret, which, once learned, will seem underwhelming. Or, maybe the effect is lost in writing because it has to be experienced.

WHAT I IF TOLD YOU, YOU READ THE FIRST LINE WRONG?
AND YOU READ THE THE SECOND PARAGRAPH WRONG TOO.

Read the text above. Did it fool you?

Maybe it did, but probably it didn't. Demonstrating magic in writing without being able to use showmanship is difficult. And, since the following is perhaps the first time you will see a magic trick demonstrated and then explained, I will make a big effort to make this a good experience for you.

A magician never reveals a secret. It's the code of conduct that we live by. Unless the secret is written in a book about magic because that shows the reader has intent and interest. Secrets are usually only revealed in resources intended for those genuinely passionate about the craft. This is why the best magic secrets are found in books, not online. Most magicians start by performing other people's tricks and effects, and when they are comfortable presenting, they create their own material, not unlike how most bands start. They start playing cover versions of other people's music, but when they go professional, it is usually with their own material. This is also how I hope you will internalize the learnings in this book. By the end of the day, use this as inspiration as you create your own way.

The effect I will describe is inspired by a magician named Harry Lorayne. I highly recommend his books if you become interested in magic throughout this book. He was a skilled magician and a master of memory and mnemonics.

Given that this is a book about magic, I feel comfortable describing a magical effect and teaching you how to perform it. It will be an effect that does not require sleight of hand.

Please perform it if you have an aspiring magician in the stomach. It will give you a taste of being on stage, doing something magical, and it might help some of the book's concepts to stand out more clearly.

Imagine this. You are giving a presentation to a large gathering. People are seated in front of you. You will demonstrate the ability to detect, under seemingly impossible conditions, who has hidden a LEGO brick in the pocket. You present this as an exercise showing the power of words and covert suggestions to influence people's actions. Yet, the audience will wonder if what they saw was a demonstration of clandestine hypnosis or reading of body language.

"Before we start, I would like you to experience something that will help set the mood," you open. "I would like to have five brave people join me here 'on stage'. The only qualification needed is that you have to be comfortable standing in front of an audience".

Whenever I get people to help me on stage, I make an effort to make them feel comfortable. Unfortunately, too many magicians and comedians make fun of the spectators to get a cheap laugh, making it more challenging to get volunteers. But, if you clearly articulate that this is a safe space, getting volunteers becomes easier. Volunteers are often described as "spectators" when describing a magic trick.

"Please stand next to each other, facing the audience," you tell them. Depending on the situation, you can ask the audience to give them a

round of applause. Some claim this conditions the audience to applaud, but I never use it, as I want any reaction to be genuine.

You introduce a red LEGO brick and hand it to one of the people on stage.

"I am now going to turn my back to you, so I cannot see what you are doing," you say as you step in front of the row of volunteers facing the audience.

"Right now, I want you to listen carefully to my instructions. Nothing should be left to chance. Or – that's actually not right. Everything should be left to chance. Listen on, as this will make perfect sense in a few moments."

As you say the above sentence, you subtly stress the words "left" and "right" when they appear in the sentence, just enough for the audience to detect that your words sound quirky and that you might be up to something.

"Now, to the person holding the brick, please hand the brick to someone standing next to you. You can pass it left or right. It is entirely up to you."

"I will turn around so I cannot see what you are doing".

You instruct the person holding the brick to hand it to either the person to the left or the person to the right. If the brick at some point is at the end, it can only travel in one direction, as the persons at the end of the row only stand next to one person.

"As a matter of fact, please do that again. You can pass it back to the person who just gave it to you or pass it further down. These are all your choices."

You repeat that two more times, ensuring that a completely random person now holds the brick.

"Now, please hide the brick somewhere on your body where I cannot see it. You can place it in your pocket or somewhere else because, in a moment, I am going to turn around".

When you turn around, it is important to do so at an angle. You never turn your back on the audience, as this will decrease the connection you are building with them.

"Please note that one of you has the brick. Not even you could have predicted who would end up having the brick, as this was a random choice made by all of your combined choices."

"Now, maybe I am reading your body language, or maybe I am reading your mind. In any case, try not to give anything away, and do not answer me verbally if I ask you a question. Understand?"

Often, they will say "yes" when you ask if they understand. You can use this for some fun by saying, *"No! I just asked you not to answer me out loud if I ask a question. You just answered 'yes'. If you want to answer, do it silently in your head, ok?"*

Sometimes, even the "ok?" will result in an audible "yes" from at least one spectator. This time, do not say anything, but look out at the audience with a subtle shrug and raising an eyebrow. This will give a different kind of laugh.

You go to one of the spectators, and with an intense stare, you ask: *"Do you have the brick? Do not answer!"*

"I'm sure you do not have the brick. Please take a seat".

You go to a second spectator (which one, I will explain below. For now, I am describing what the audience sees.

"Do you have the brick? Do not answer. At least not loud. You can answer in your mind. But feel free to lie or tell the truth."

After some dramatic acting from your side, you dismiss a second spectator and are now left with three people on stage.

"As I turn my back again, please make one final pass of the brick to someone so we can start from a clean slate. I might have picked up a clue or two, so let's make this even more difficult".

You turn around and look at the audience, allowing the volunteers to move the brick a final time unseen by you. When they're done, you return to face them. Remember not to have your back towards the audience, but stand at an angle.

You lower your voice and say, slowly:

"Now, the person who has the brick suddenly starts to feel like there's a weight on your shoulders. You are carrying this weight. It is tough. Heavy. The two of you not holding the brick will feel light, as if helium balloons were tied to you. It's light. Easy. As I speak these words, you will feel light. Almost floating. You will look up."

You are saying those words in a deep, hypnotic voice. You do not have to be trained in hypnosis to do this. As a matter of fact, it's more fun if you're not because then you will enjoy even more when you occasionally get a clear response from these words, turning them from pseudo-hypnosis into actual hypnotic words. If you can clearly see from the reactions who has the brick, take a bow and the recognition as not only a magician but also, apparently, a master hypnotist. Sometimes, the person holding the brick will clearly look like they are carrying a weight, while the others will stand up straight.

This happens occasionally, but fear not – you know exactly who has the brick. The above sentence is merely part of the act, and it has nothing to do with the method. In most cases, you will not get a physical reaction to this pseudo-hypnosis, so you continue:

*"Now, did you notice how I directed your choices when I said **right** now nothing is **left** to chance? Sorry to have deceived you, but I am not reading body language. I influenced all of your choices by covertly placing commands in my instructions, and your subconscious hopefully got these instructions, even if you didn't notice them consciously".*

Now the audience might remember the quirkiness when you gave the instructions. They will not remember exactly how many times you said "right" and "left", so they cannot backtrack the method. This is good because it is another layer of pseudo-explanation. You did not influence them, but you are pretending to use a real, existing method that takes years of practice to master. You will learn how to do this for real in a later chapter.

Now is the time to build some suspense.

"That's why I know you don't have the brick, and neither do you. Please take a seat".

You instruct two of the three spectators to take a seat, leaving just one person with you.

"I really hope this is going to work. I have no idea if I made a mistake, and you are all excellent at not giving away any subtle cues".

"If I managed to influence your subconsciousness covertly, you have the brick. Please hand me the brick and return to your seat", you say to the last spectator.

You say these words as you approach the spectator whom you have correctly identified as holding the brick. As the spectators return to their seats, you hold up the brick for everyone to see. This is what is known as an "applause position". Often, audiences are not aware of when and where they should applaud. Different performance arts have different unwritten rules. In opera, applauding after an aria, a duet, or other significant vocal or instrumental pieces within the performance is customary. However, it is generally considered inappropriate to clap during the recitatives – the narrative-like sections that connect the more elaborate musical pieces. During a classical music concert, it is customary to wait until the end before applauding—this means waiting for all the movements of a symphony or a concerto to be performed. In some cases, the conductor might turn to face the audience to signal that it is time to applaud. Audiences appreciates applause cues, and you will often get bigger applauses if they know it is okay to do so.

Now let's dive into how you know who has the brick. If you haven't already guessed, the method has nothing to do with body language or spoken language. It's something else, and here is the explanation.

I AM NOT A NUMBER, I AM A FREE MAN

Let us number the five spectators from left to right. The leftmost spectator is number 1 up to the rightmost who is number 5.

You initially hand the brick to spectator number 2. The reason is presumably so that the person can hand the brick both to the right and to the left when the trick starts. Had you given the brick to spectator number 1, the only possibility would be to hand it to the right. So giving it to spectator 2 makes it fairer.

You can choose to say this explicitly, but I found that it is not necessary. You just haphazardly hand it to the second spectator, thinking the above.

Just to be clear: The reason for giving the brick to the second spectator is part of the method, not to make it fairer. Here's why it works:

If you follow the script above, the brick will be passed from person to person *four* times.

After passing the brick from person to person four times, it can only end up with either spectator number 2 or in the hands of spectator number 4. You do not know which of them has it, but it is still good information that you can use, as you now know that neither the first nor the last person can possibly have the brick.

Most people assume that, at this point, the brick can be in the hands of any one of the five spectators due to the seemingly random process.

That means the two spectators you will discard in the first phase are placed at positions 1 and 5, respectively. As you pretend to read each spectator, remember the showmanship part of the act. Be an actor who can do what you pretend you can do.

By now, you have sent two spectators back to their seats. There are three people still with you. You do not know who has the brick. Yet.

"I might have picked up a few clues when I was talking to you before, so to make this even more fair, I will turn my back, and you will do one last pass. Whoever has the brick, hand it to someone left or right of you."

You are actually doing the exact opposite of what you are communicating. This does not make it fairer. On the contrary, this sequence ensures that the brick ends up in the hand of spectator number 3.

It is a thing of terrifying beauty, as the great mentalist Max Maven used to say.

The act of seemingly making this fairer deliberately puts the brick in the hand of spectator 3. We set this up in the previous act of making the trick more impossible, as the passing of the brick four times places it in the hands of either spectator 2 or 4.

THAT MEANS, WHOEVER HAS IT, CAN ONLY DO ONE THING – HAND IT TO THE PERSON IN THE MIDDLE – SPECTATOR 3.

It is, indeed, a thing of terrifying beauty.

From here on out, all you have to do is follow the script and dial up on your showmanship. You know exactly who has the brick.

The more you engage the audience in the "reading" of the spectators, the more engagement you get. Think of it as drawing imaginary lines between the people seated in front of you, and the stage area. Turn to them and ask *"did you also see the eye movements when I asked her if she was lying?"* or *"Notice how he shifted his weight from one foot to the other?"*. Often, the audience will react and shout out their own observations, making the trick even better.

I came up with the method for this trick after seeing a card trick by the beforementioned Harry Lorayne when we met many years ago. I wanted to do something without cards, though. It had to involve people and engage the audience in a way that did not seem like a magic trick but like a feat of mental ability.

I started backwards. That is, I began the development of the trick with how it would look to the spectators. I wanted to be able to detect which among them was holding a brick. How I would accomplish that would have to wait – a good trick begins with the effect first and the method later. Other magicians have come up with similar methods, and some have made the effect even stronger[73].

Plenty of tricks demonstrate that, as a magician, you can get the outcome you want – when performing a trick. But what if you are not doing a magic trick? Can you still get what you want?

YOU CAN'T ALWAYS GET WHAT YOU WANT

USE THE FORCE LUKE

In my leadership, I have a mental model of how I want to lead and how I would prefer to be led. It is a three-step model called "the three I's". It begins with "inspire". I hope that what I do inspires people. Inspire them to do what is right, without me being specific about what to do precisely, nor what "the right thing" is. The more specific you are in your leadership, the more you limit curiosity. Who knows – maybe the employee will dream up something amazing that I hadn't thought about. Catch a magical rabbit that I would have missed.

The next step is the "instruct" step. Already here, we are putting constraints onto the employee that are not enabling but governing constraints. Instructing an employee to do something is a signal that something in the system is not functioning. It may be the employee that lacks capabilities or just doesn't find the work inspiring, but it may also be something else. When instructing, I always take time to reflect on why it was necessary to do so.

The last step is "insist". Now, if you tried to inspire the employee in vain and instructing them didn't help, you sometimes have to resort to insisting as a leader. After all, it is within your powers as a leader to do so. It says a lot about the system when a leader has to insist. Is there enough psychological safety, so the employee would feel comfortable saying why the work wasn't done and why the leader had to insist?

INSPIRE, INSTRUCT, INSIST.

Leadership is a broad role. You lead your organization and your business, but other actors are also in the system, such as vendors, customers, officials, etc. The three-step model works primarily within your organization. Outside your organization, leadership happens through another "i" step.

INFLUENCE.

Influence is all about giving someone the illusion of free choice when they, in essence, do precisely what you want. Influence is governed by ethics, and in this section, we will discuss influence and ethics in relationship to leadership.

Magicians give spectators the illusion of free choice all the time.

"Pick a card, any card."

Here's the thing. You will pick exactly the card I want you to pick, giving you only the illusion of "any card."

What I say is: *"Pick a card, any card."*

What I think is: *"Pick a card, this card."*

In the language of magicians, we call this "a force." When we force a card, we call it "card force." When we force a thought, we call it "psychological force." There are other words and entire taxonomies – for instance, in the article "A Psychologically Based Taxonomy of Magicians' Forcing Techniques: How magicians influence our choices, and how to use this to study psychological mechanisms[74]." Most of the science and articles are written by laymen (a term magicians use for people who are not magicians – akin to "muggle" from the Harry Potter™ universe). The advantage is that it is unbiased reading, but that is also the disadvantage. If you have never been on a stage, and your applause is 100% dependent on you making a spectator think of the specific word that you have written on a piece of paper, sealed in an envelope, then there's a chance you've missed the finer details.

Most psychological forces are based on the words we say. We carefully construct sentences and instructions that sound fair to the untrained ear but will control the audience's choices. That is the basis of most prediction effects where the magician asks the spectator some seemingly fair and open questions, yet the magician predicted everything at the end of the trick.

We can't really predict the future, but as the saying goes: *"The easiest way to predict the future is to create it"*.

As a mentalist with thousands of shows behind me, I effortlessly control other people's choices on stage. As with every other skill, it is something to be honed and trained through repetition. Being on stage clearly articulating "I will now control your mind" has given me an excellent base for practicing this particular skill in an ethical and safe environment.

But how is influencing other people's choices different from manipulation?

As a curiosity, it is very different from manipulation in the magic world. Manipulation means "to move by hand." The magician practices manipulation when you see a stage magician producing cards or coins from thin air. It is a common thing in magic, and there are even competitions in manipulation.

To a magician, manipulation is a neutral word. It is not associated with anything good or bad. It is also not associated with the type of mind control and the psychological forces a mentalist uses.

Assuming the leader has the skills to do it, is it the prerogative of a leader to influence/manipulate an employee? Is it mitigating circumstances if we claim it is in the employee's best interest?

Let's answer that one part at a time.

It is the prerogative of a leader to change the working conditions of the employee – even if it is not in the employee's best interest. Otherwise, we could never let an employee go. That is the leader influencing the employee, and it is probably not in the employee's best interest. But it is still part of the job to fire someone if there are good reasons to do so.

On the other hand, it is not the job of a leader to covertly influence/nudge/manipulate an employee to do anything, not even if it is in the employee's best interest.

Who are we, as leaders, to be the judge of what is best for the employee?

Here's a story from someone I was coaching. Let's call him Ben, and he was feeling guilty.

"I just knew Joan was a talent and that she was meant for something big." he began at our first session.

"I remember when I was a junior account manager, all I wanted was to be a senior account manager and end up a director. I worked hard for it, which took me a long time. Looking at Joan, I could see she was in the same place. I invited her boss for lunch, spoke highly of Joan, and said he wouldn't regret it if he promoted her. When she made Senior Account Manager, I continued my clandestine activities, helping her on the way to Account Director. I felt so good about myself that I never told her I was doing these things. She thought it was all her own doing, and I was not the one to ruin that belief. It gave her self-confidence, I'm sure."

As Ben was talking, it became clear that he had seen himself as Joan's guardian angel, helping her get the promotions in record time. He had used all his powers as a leader, influencing Joan and her surroundings and having her best interest in mind.

When Joan quit after having been away for many months due to stress, Ben was getting an epiphany. Joan explained on her last day that she had a rather fragile personality. Her dream job was Junior Account Manager with limited responsibilities, giving her time for her garden and her dog.

She never wanted those promotions, nor did she desire them. Ben had projected his own desire on her, and his bias had caused him to do harm, even if he thought he did something good.

I only changed the story slightly for this example, changing only the names and the job titles. I got permission from both Ben and Joan to include the story, as they both agreed it carries an important point. It is, by the way, a common misconception that leaders think everybody wants to be a leader[75].

You never know what is in the best interest of the employee. Nudging, manipulating, and influencing is not something you can do with their best interest in mind.

Instead, you can create the space for them to grab the opportunities if they so desire. But the ambition to move is theirs, not yours. And this is the difference from manipulation, which literally means to move by hand. You can create the conditions to move towards something, but the action has to be theirs, not yours.

In some countries, there is a law term called the "bonus pater" – the good father. It is a fictional person that would act reasonably and good in any situation. Lawyers could say, *"are the defendant's actions similar to that of a bonus pater?"* It was a way to set the bar of good behavior without defining it in detail but simply create an image of someone good, whom everyone could somehow imagine.

If we introduce a similar term – *"bonus princeps"* – the good leader – are there any situations where the bonus princeps would manipulate a colleague?

Assuming the answer is "no – the bonus princeps would never resort to manipulation", is then knowledge of covert influence, mind control, and manipulation evil? Or is it, on the contrary, a necessity as it helps you identify when someone tries to manipulate you? Think of it as learning a martial art. Not because you want to attack but because you want to defend.

In that spirit, I will let you in on some of the secrets of magic that can be used – and abused – so please, think as the bonus princeps would.

You will learn how to manipulate the fabric of time itself, allowing you to stop time at your will. You will learn how the brain reacts to different inputs, allowing you to hack the brain into seeing something else. These powers should only be known by the bonus princeps. If you are a leader thinking, "oh great, I can use these techniques to manipulate my way to success", know that science tells us that manipulative leaders do not have any advantage in pursuing power at work[76].

As the famous physicist Richard Feynman said at Caltech in 1974: "The first principle is that you must not fool yourself – and you are the easiest person to fool" in a speech about the importance of honesty and integrity in scientific research, and he cautioned his listeners not to deceive themselves or others in their pursuit of knowledge.

The book "Foolproof: Why Misinformation Infects Our Minds and How to Build Immunity[77]" suggests that knowing about manipulation techniques acts as a vaccine and helps builds immunity towards information that others want to present to you as true. Assuming that is true, the next chapter will boost your mental immune system.

A MOMENTARY LAPSE OF REASON

Learn how to control
the fabric of time and how to become

INVISIBLE

The previous chapter discussed the 3+1 leadership model (Inspire, instruct, insist + influence) and the ethics governing influence. For the sake of completion, we will take a step deeper into the magical world of **influence.**

As I was writing this chapter, I found myself experiencing cognitive dissonance.

On the one hand, I was aware of the potential for the information to be abused and used in ways that violate the rights and dignity of others. On the other hand, I also knew that the same information and techniques could be used for good to improve people's lives and build stronger, more harmonious communities. I realized that I couldn't control how the readers would use the information and that the responsibility for ethical behavior ultimately lies with the individual.

However, I also believe that providing guidance and setting a positive example is essential. I hope that by emphasizing the importance of ethical behavior throughout this chapter, readers will be inspired to use the information to benefit themselves and others.

Here's a simple example of how to influence another person using your words. In my magic show, I have a piece where I guess in which hand a spectator is holding a coin. I do that three times in a row to demonstrate that it was not just a fluke the first time. After guessing correctly the first time, I ask the spectator to put their hands behind their back and secretly put the coin in either hand. I then say: *"You have a completely free choice. You can pick any hand you want, but I'm telling you already now, that you will pick the left hand."*

Now think about the influence these words have on the spectator. At first, they will think, *"Aha – he wants me to put the coin in my left hand. I'm going to put it in the right hand. That'll teach him!"*

Then, after a split second, the spectator will think: *"Baloney! That's what he wants me to do. I will leave it in the left. That'll teach him!"*

And soon thereafter, the spectator, now feeling cognitive dissonance, will think: *"That will make me seem like a pushover. I'll put it in the right hand!"*

As you can see, this simple sentence influences the spectator's choice profoundly.

Influencing others is a powerful tool that can be used to achieve great things, whether in the workplace, in relationships, or the community. However, it is essential to remember that with great power comes great responsibility.

It is important to me that the techniques presented in this chapter are used ethically, with respect for the rights and dignity of others. This chapter aims to provide readers with the knowledge and skills they need to influence others in an effective and morally sound way. We will explore the importance of being transparent and acting with integrity, all of which are essential for ethical influence. By learning and applying these techniques, readers will be able to achieve their goals while maintaining the respect and trust of those around them.

Let's begin with a secret of magic that I don't mind sharing, as it has a section in Wikipedia.

When magicians make a coin vanish, we use a technique called "retention of vision." The human brain has this exceptional capability to "fill in the blanks."

That is, it creates images in our brains that are not real.

For instance, we cannot see when our eyes move. Try for yourself and look in a mirror and see if you can see your eyes moving. Our brain is doing what is called saccadic masking. It shuts off the processing of retinal images while the eye moves, then travel back in time, creating artificial images to fill in the blanks instead of just showing the brain blank images.

It is almost like a mathematical interpolation. Given a starting image (just before the blackout happens) and an end image (just after the vision is restored), the brain interpolates the images that would have been there had we not been effectively blind. The brain does this all the time, with different methods. While saccadic masking is done through memory, the blind spot is filled out through the construction of sensory input from the other eye – for the most part. People who are blind on one eye will still not see the blind spot, but the brain compensates through other means.

Our peripheral vision covers a wide field of view, but the resolution and acuity are much lower compared to our central vision. This means that objects in the peripheral vision are less well-defined and less distinct. However, the brain uses the information from the peripheral vision in conjunction with information from the central vision to create a seamless visual perception of the environment. It fills in missing details, interprets shapes, and predicts what will likely be present in the visual field. This allows us to maintain a stable and continuous perception of the world around us, even when our gaze is moving or we're moving ourselves. It is not just visual that the brain fills in the blanks, it also does the same with sound, as in the case of the missing fundamental illusion[78], or haptic feelings such as the rubber hand illusion[79].

Not all creatures have the capability of filling in the blanks. If you look at pigeons or chickens when they walk, they move their head forward, and then the rest of the body follows while they keep the head still. Their eyes are on the side of the head, and if they didn't move like that, everything would be a blur, like watching out of the window of a fast-moving train.

Magicians know about saccadic masking, and we use (some would say abuse) this fact. We know when the spectator, for all intent and purposes, is completely blind. During that period, we can do whatever we want, as we are invisible in the purest sense of the word. We cannot be seen.

Not only do we have an (albeit limited) period where we can act unseen, but we can also manipulate what images the brain creates to fill in the blank. This is the "retention of vision" vanish that we use to make a coin seemingly disappear in front of our very eyes. If the coin is the last image the retina can detect, it will be the first image of the interpolation, and therefore it will be part of the image generated by the brain attempting to fill in the blank. Watching a skilled coin magician is almost mesmerizing because the coins do, for all intent and purposes, disappear and re-appear as if by magic.

The context of eliciting saccadic masking does not have to be a magic trick. As a leader and decision-maker, people will try to influence you. And, if they know the secret of stopping time, you could be defenseless if you do not know it exists.

Once, I heard rumors about someone who could make parts of a presentation invisible. The audience couldn't see it, yet when shown a video of the presentation afterward, it was clearly there all the time. It turned out he was a con man (at least from my perspective), showing people one thing, yet they perceived something else. I did get a chance to watch a video recording of him, and I immediately recognized the shenanigans, which I will now explain so you will not fall for this ruse.

Before you read this sentence, could you feel your watch, glasses, or socks? Assuming that you are wearing one of those items. If not, did you ever notice that your nose is blocking parts of your vision?

Known as **Troxler's Fading**[80], it is a fascinating optical illusion that has been known for centuries. It is a phenomenon in which an unchanging, isolated (visual) stimulus eventually disappears from our perception, even though it remains physically present in the visual field. When our eyes are exposed to a static, unchanging visual stimulus, our brains tend to filter it out and stop actively processing it.

This phenomenon is thought to be related to the way that our brains regulate the flow of sensory information, allowing us to focus on what is most important or relevant in our environment. The previously mentioned conman abused this to hide what would previously have been "the small print" in plain sight. By having a presentation with lots of animations, movements, and colors, the information he was bound by law to present was held static at the same place on the screen while all the bells and whistles were floating around. This meant that when people eventually sued him for fraud, he could say that he had disclosed all information beforehand.

With the increased use of audio-visual presentations, creating momentary lapses of reason is easier than ever. If you experience it, it might not be done with malicious intent – it can be just a creative ploy used to make a presentation more impactful.

Constructing a presentation like this is part craft, part art. The crafting part comes in when setting up. The presenter must know the room's layout and the attendees' position beforehand. The audio/video parts of the presentation intended to plant false images or elicit saccadic masking need intensive testing on real audiences. Using this for anything else but entertainment and using it on unsuspecting participants is unethical, and you need to know when someone is trying to pull a stunt on you.

Most people have experienced momentary lapses of reason. You may find yourself driving home after a long day at work, only to realize that you have missed your exit on the highway and have been driving on autopilot. Or you may be reading a book and suddenly realize you have lost track of what you have been reading. If you can recall that feeling, that is how you feel if someone has used this technique on you. Of course, you could also just have been daydreaming, so do not attribute the feeling to malicious intent but as an indicator of an awareness point.

Knowing the science behind the technique is not enough to perform it but enough to recognize it. I can distinguish Mozart from Bach on the radio, but I am in no way proficient in playing either Mozart or Bach on my piano.

Let me just repeat, once again, that ethical behavior is essential. Whilst I want you to know about a secret weapon you probably did not know existed, there is a chance that this will be read by someone with a lower ethical threshold than me, and I would be loathe to give such an impactful persuasion technique to the wrong person. Ultimately, how you use this information is for you to decide. Choose wisely.

With that out of the way, let's explore how to introduce new objects into play, making the audience believe they are well-known objects.

Magic and mentalism are an illusion. What you see is carefully crafted to represent something real that can do something imaginary. It is more magical to witness an ordinary coin disappear into thin air than an object you've never seen before because you are quite familiar with the physical properties of a coin.

Often, magicians use what is known as skeuomorphism to further the illusion. A skeuomorphic object is a new or unknown object created in such a way that it mimics something existing and well-known. Magicians refer to these objects as "gimmicks," "props," or "MacGuffins." The concept of skeuomorphism is not limited to magic and can be used in communication and persuasion, but first, let's be clear on what it achieves.

Skeuomorphism played an essential role in adopting the new technology called a light bulb, replacing the old gas lamp[81]. Allegedly, people were used to gas lights and were reluctant to switch to electricity. Yet, the transformation was fast, and the entire Fifth Avenue was electrified entirely within a decade[82]. To make the change seem smaller, Edison limited the light bulb efficiency to 13 watts, not to outshine the gas lamp, which was approximately 13 watts. Gas lamps had a cover to keep them from spattering. The light bulb did not leak, but Edison added a lampshade to make the lamps look similar. The lamp shades initially had no other purpose than to enable skeuomorphism. Later, they became part of the design and style as a decorative element, and much later, they started to serve the purpose of diffusing and softening the light.

When the mechanical relay in blinker switches in a car was replaced with an electronic switch, the car manufacturers added a small loudspeaker playing the sound of a relay going on and off because people were used to that sound.

We hear an artificial shutter sound when our smartphone takes a picture, and the icon for making a call is that of an old-fashioned rotary phone handset. We saw skeuomorphism when the electric car made its entry. The charging cable could be anywhere, but the initial chargers were at the same place as the gasoline opening, and the charging cable-connector looked like a gasoline pump-handle.

While these examples are audio-visual, there is no limit to the usage: Using "chocolate" in "white chocolate" even though there are no roasted cacao beans in white chocolate, technically, it is not even chocolate. Or naming a new and unknown game invented in Germany "Chinese Checkers," to make it sound familiar in the marketing material, even though it was not from China nor had anything to do with checkers. Notice that verbal skeuomorphism requires intent, just as the visual do. That's why "Westminister Abbey" is not a skeuomorphism, even though it ceased being an abbey half a millennium ago.

THE PURPOSE OF MAKING THE COMMUNICATION EASY TO INTERNALIZE IS FOR THE RECIPIENT TO MAKE UP THEIR OWN REASONS WHY IT IS A GOOD IDEA.

The concept goes by the name of self-generated arguments and is generally thought to be more persuasive than adapting other people's arguments[83].

Introducing ideas as the recipient's own or something the recipient is already familiar with will increase the adoption and acceptance of these ideas. Masking out common objection points and hiding weaknesses in plain sight will further increase adoption. This behavior is seen most often in negotiations and in sales.

While the elements have been presented as discrete or singular methods, the practical utilization is intended to be fluent and continuous, seamlessly blending into each other.

The science of magical language is much more affluent, and we'll take a closer look at the magical language in the next chapter.

SPEAKING WORDS OF WISDOM

Learn a language

WITHIN THE LANGUAGE

"Pick a card, any card," I tell the next spectator. "And just as in the last trick, you are free to exchange the card for another one." I continue my patter. Patter or patterline is what magicians call the part of a trick that is scripted. That is, we are very precise and deliberate in what we are saying instead of ad-libbing.

The trick I am about to perform is called "Ambitious card," where a card keeps jumping to the top of the deck, despite being shuffled into the middle. It is a popular trick, and it is based on sleight of hand alone. That means the card selected is not forced – it's genuinely a free choice.

In the trick I use prior to this one, the card is forced. That is, the spectator picks exactly the card I want. Despite appearances, the above patterline is actually not about the current trick. It is designed instead to reinforce the previous trick. By suggesting that they can exchange the card "just like in the last trick," I place a memory in their head that is not real. I'm using language to enhance the magic effects by using imaginary language.

Before I decided to focus fully on mentalism, I was a close-up magician. I usually performed at banquets or parties where the audience sat at tables, enjoying a meal. I would walk from table to table, doing sleight-of-hand magic with cards and coins. Let's say there are 30 tables at an average show, and so with 2-5 shows per weekend, I would perform several hundred times per weekend. That gave me ample opportunity to hone my language skills and perfect the creation of verbal illusions.

> ## WORDS WERE ORIGINALLY MAGIC, AND THE WORD RETAINS MUCH OF ITS OLD MAGICAL POWER EVEN TODAY. WITH WORDS, ONE MAN CAN MAKE ANOTHER MAN BLESSED OR DRIVE HIM TO DESPAIR.
>
> *SIGMUND FREUD,*
> *INTRODUCTORY LECTURES ON PSYCHOANALYSIS*

Remember the analogy of mathematics. How complex numbers are a sum of real and imaginary numbers. By adding the imaginary number, we get a whole new dimension in which we can travel.

Magical language works in the same way. We may talk about something in the present, but it will influence the past or the future. A good magic patter is designed to set up a future effect or increase a past. It will fly by most spectators, as they believe we talk about the present, as most conversations usually do.

Let's look at an example. I will try to make the example in normal language, as the magic lingo might be confusing.

The sentence, "Morgan got the milk from the refrigerator," only makes sense if:

Milk exists.
Milk is in the fridge.
Milk is in a container, not just poured out at the fridge's bottom.
The fridge exists.
Morgan exists.
Morgan is a human (i.e., we assume Morgan is not a dog).
And so forth.

Epistemologically speaking, these assumptions are called presuppositions. The same word is used in the pragmatic field of linguistics to describe what we silently assume to be true to make meaning.

We are used to accepting presuppositions. Otherwise, our dialogues would be endlessly tiresome. We can accept that someone says, "Taylor opened the door," without asking: "Ok, so just to confirm. Taylor has hands? And the door has a handle?" etc.

Presuppositions are the name for all the things we silently and automatically accept as true for a sentence to make sense.

PRESUPPOSITIONS ARE A POWERFUL TOOL.

Advertisers have known about this for a long time. There was a brand of beef that was not selling as well as the competitors. Their meat was pale in color, while the competitor's meat had an appetizing red color. They were both found next to each other in the supermarket's freezer. How did they win market share? By adding a big sticker on the foil package with the words: "Contains no artificial color!". Now, when customers saw these two next to each other, they assumed that the colorful meat contained artificial color. Otherwise, the presence of the sticker wouldn't make sense. The sticker created a presupposition – and an unethical one nonetheless.

We have to take presuppositions for granted to have meaningful dialogues.

We never think about the presuppositions present in our sentences. We only think about what we want to communicate and do not think about the presuppositions we inadvertently create – unless we can speak a magical language.

Magical language is the sum of the real and the imaginary. The real part of the sentence is that Morgan actually got some milk.

The imaginary part of the sentence is all the presuppositions that we now accept as true.

IMAGINE THAT. A LANGUAGE WITHIN OUR LANGUAGE THAT PASSES ALL SCRUTINY AND DISCUSSION AND IS ACCEPTED AS FACT. A LANGUAGE YOU ALREADY UNDERSTAND BUT THAT YOU DO NOT YET SPEAK.

Remember the example of Kim, who had an employee – Joshua – a low performer with a toxic attitude, constantly threatening to quit.

We used that example to demonstrate "Illusion language" – a method for figuring out what is real and what is imagined. This is how Kim learned about Mary, who was skilled in "magical language." Mary was the product manager on the team, and Kim had 1:1 sessions with her twice a month. Mary did not like Joshua because he challenged her decisions, and she wanted to hurt his narrative.

"Joshua's performance is getting better," Mary said. While that at first read might sound like a compliment, several presuppositions exist in the sentence. One of them is that John's performance had to be bad – or worse than it is now – to make sense.

"I have spent a lot of time coaching Joshua, and I'm happy to report that he is not threatening to quit." Mary continues.

"I haven't spent enough time on Joshua, though, because I have been dealing with toxic behavior from another team member." Mary is humble and talks about her inadequacy. Or so we think. Mary can easily take this very small hit on her abilities as a coach in order for her to suggest via presuppositions that Joshua's behavior is toxic. As she is saying the sentence, she stresses the "another team member" such that it becomes evident that it is not Joshua's behavior this time. However, the presupposition in the sentence is that Joshua is displaying toxic

behavior, and it is still there because she has not spent enough time coaching him as she deemed necessary.

The way you stress a word in a sentence creates meaning to the sentence. Let's look at an example:

"I LOVE YOU".

I LOVE YOU – IT IS ME THAT LOVES YOU, NOT SOMEONE ELSE.

I **LOVE** YOU – I FEEL LOVE, NOT HATE OR INDIFFERENCE.

I LOVE **YOU** – IT IS YOU THAT I LOVE, NOT SOMEONE ELSE.

This is called **prosody**, and we will explore the finer details in a later chapter. For now, it suffices that you know how stressing a word can change the meaning of a sentence. You might want to read the example line out loud to get the knack.

Mary honed her skills when she was in sales. She would say things like: *"Do you know if it's the low price of our product that makes you interested in buying it?"* to a potential customer. She places the idea that the price is low. If the customer says "No!" Mary would continue:

"No? Well, that's perfectly normal – many of our customers want to buy it not due to the low price but the fine quality." Mary changes something negative – a "no" to something positive by answering with another presupposition that the product is of high quality.

Mary would continue: *"Are you excited due to the vast possibilities or the flexibility of our product?"*

For that question to make sense, the customer is now excited. The product has vast possibilities and is apparently flexible. Mary is not directly saying that – she presupposes it. Look at the number of presuppositions she could cram into a single sentence.

Let's say Mary has malicious intent and wants to subconsciously plant the idea of Joshua tripping over something and falling. She can't just say, *"I hope you trip and fall!"* – Joshua would notice that and just disregard it.

Try to ask a question. *"Should I go up the stairs?"*. Ask it out loud and listen to your voice. Notice how the pitch increases at the end of the sentence. This is called question intonation.

Now say it as a command. *"Go up the stairs!"* Notice that now your pitch decreases at the end of the sentence. This is called declarative intonation.

If you ask anyone to guess if you are asking a question or saying a command, they would guess correctly, even if your words were just mumbo jumbo. We are primed to understand commands and questions based on intonation.

"*Go up the stairs?*" sounds different to "*Go up the stairs!*" even if they are the same words. You can immediately recognize the question from the command.

Now imagine if Mary simply says: "Hey – have a nice *trip* this *fall*." and says the words trip and fall with a downward pitch. Joshua would hear the reality, a nice wish, but he would also hear, but not notice, the commands to trip and fall.

The scary thing about commands hidden in the language is that it works with homonyms and homophones. That is, words sound the same but might be spelled differently. "Week" sounds exactly like "weak". "Accept" and "except". "Cue" and "queue." If you use this clandestine commanding method, the subconscious does not care about spelling.

Mary's favorite example is: *"If you think about this product, by now you have probably made up your mind."* Using the downwards pitch on "by" "now" "this" and "product", creating the command: *"Buy this product now!"*

There is a variation of this technique known as Embedded Commands[84]. I have not had much luck with those, but if you find this area interesting, there is a reference to further reading in the endnotes.

Planting commands and thoughts into the mind of someone is not just something magicians do to create an immersive and exciting magic show. As we have seen, the techniques can be used outside the entertainment arena.

In 1974, psychologist Elizabeth Loftus did some interesting experiments about altering people's memories. Specifically, she studied how witnesses in a courtroom could be manipulated through language[85].

The most well-known experiment was to show the same footage of two cars colliding and then slightly change the wording of the questions. *"About how fast were the cars going when they smashed/collided/bumped/hit/contacted each other."* Elizabeth's results were quite clear – the estimated velocity increased by the wording used to describe the incident.

Clearly, "smashed" presupposes a faster speed than "bumped".

Given this experiment's precise and repeatable results, she continued to ask, *"How much broken glass did you see?"*. There was no broken glass in the footage, but for the participant to make sense of the question, they had to presuppose that there was broken glass. As with the speed experiment, the more powerful word used to describe the speed, the more glass they reported seeing.

Using presuppositions to plant false memories is also used in therapy. Or the other way around – identifying a false memory that acts as a limiting belief of the client and removing the memory. The evidence of false memories shared by a group of people is examined in the 2022 study "The Visual Mandela Effect as evidence for shared and specific false memories across people[86]."

At the beginning of the chapter, we asserted that knowledge of language and influence techniques could be used in self-defense. An example is the following quote from a US presidential election, where a candidate turned a negative image into a positive one purely using language.

"I will not make age an issue of this campaign. I am not going to exploit, for political purposes, my opponent's youth and inexperience", Ronald Reagan quipped during the 1984 presidential debates when asked if, at 73, he was too old to be President. Regan turned the question around and used it to make an awareness point about his opponent's inexperience.

Similarly, attacks can be hidden in a defense. In another presidential debate, Nixon wanted to use the fact that there had never been a Catholic president in the USA. Kennedy was a catholic, and Nixon wanted to bring this to the voters' attention without seeming to be attacking Kennedy or Catholicism. He said:

"I don't want anyone not to vote for John Kennedy because he is a Catholic."

Language is powerful. When magicians create their manuscript – called a "patterline"- one golden rule is applied to every single word.

"If it does not add, it subtracts." Every word is scrutinized, and if it does not add to the effect, it is removed. That doesn't mean a patterline should be dense or dry. Creating engagement and delight is also an outcome, so there will be words in a patterline whose purpose is to set the mood or increase engagement. It is not all about the effect or the bottom line. The language is always holistic to the overall purpose.

It is often helpful to create a manuscript, even if you do not follow it to the letter. Following the audience's reactions is more important than following your manuscript. Manuscript writing forces you to consider the purpose of every single word, and after a while, it will become second nature, and you can do it on the fly while speaking.

LANGUAGE IS THE MAGIC YOU CREATE. IT IS THE INTERFACE BETWEEN IMAGINATION AND REALITY. WHEN YOU ARE ON STAGE DOING YOUR TOWN HALL PRESENTATION, THINK ABOUT YOUR LANGUAGE AS A LEADER.

Whether the people I address are spectators at a magic show or employees from my business unit, I find it beneficial to create a sense of belonging and increase their awareness for maximum learning. Luckily, our dear brain has just the right drug for that. Dopamine enhances learning, motivation, and attention, while oxytocin creates that feeling of relatedness that has earned it the nickname "the empathy hormone." Together with endorphins – our 'feel-good' chemicals – our brain is perfectly capable of creating the best environment for your messages to be well received, whether in business or entertainment.

There is an emotion that triggers all those neurotransmitters. The emotion is laughter, and a variety of feelings can trigger it.

Feelings and emotions are not the same things. We can laugh when we are nervous and cry when we are happy. We can joke and laugh to mask discomfort. Emotions are non-voluntary signals that can be hard to control. This is why emotions are used in, for instance, lie detection because you can't control the expressions on your face.

Emotions are physical – the "motion" part of the word already tells us that.

We don't just want the emotion; we want the feeling. That's why it's not enough to simply tell a funny joke. It creates the same level of belonging as one would feel towards the newspaper while reading a joke from the funny pages. Creating the right level of laughter based on the right feelings is an art you should consider mastering.

THE MOST BEAUTIFUL THING WE CAN EXPERIENCE IS THE MYSTERIOUS.

ALBERT EINSTEIN

This is not a section about humor, and I would encourage you to avoid just telling a joke. While a joke can elicit an emotional response, it is like eating a piece of candy to get energy. A short burst of energy that will quickly evaporate. Laughing can come from feelings and moods; solid, well-grounded laughter can be quite bonding. I have a sequence in my show that I know will generate a huge amount of heartwarming laughter. I ask a spectator to think of a random word, not writing it down and not telling anyone. I then proceed to read the spectator's mind, revealing the word. The directness of the demonstration of mind reading never fails to get the audience to laugh in disbelief. "That's impossible!?" they gasp between laughter. Had they known that the word I was "reading" was planted deliberately by me a few moments before, the reaction would, of course, be different.

THIS IS WHY MAGICIANS GUARD THEIR SECRETS – BECAUSE THEY HELP BUILD FEELINGS AND ELICIT EMOTIONS.

This section is part of the chapter on "magical language" because I use the psycholinguistic models of language to create captivating and emotional narratives. I am neither the inventor of psycholinguistics nor of the application to elicit arousal in emotions[87].

As the old saying goes: **"People may forget what you said, but they will not forget how you made them feel"**. This is a powerful quote –

so powerful that a lot of people claim to be the first to have said it. To my knowledge, this goes back to Carl Buehner.

I use language to build up expectations. But then, just as the crescendo has been built up, I change the tune to something else. The philosopher Immanuel Kant once said: *"In everything that is to excite a lively convulsive laugh, there must be something absurd[88]."* Coincidentally, absurd comes from Latin absurdus, meaning "out of tune". Let's explore how to get out of tune with magic:

One of the first sleight-of-hand card tricks I did was to take a shuffled deck of cards, do some fancy cuts, and produce the Ace of Spades. Then, I would do a one-handed swivel cut, produce the Ace of Diamonds, and continue producing the Ace of Clubs. Then, while the three aces are face down on the table, I do a fancy card fan, and a card shoots out of the deck. I catch it between my fingers and show... The Queen of Hearts.

"That's unfortunate," I signal with my body language without saying anything, looking at the three face-down cards. Then I wave the Queen over the cards and turn them over to show the other remaining Queens, having successfully produced the four queens from the deck. The aces? Oh – please look under the card case.

This effect is much more powerful than simply producing the four aces because of the contrast between what the audience expects and what they see. Coincidentally, it makes switching each Ace for a Queen much easier, because no one is looking or expecting me to switch those cards.

After the third ace production, the audience knows what to expect. They get the tune. By producing a Queen, and then showing that the other three produced cards are now queens, the tune – all of a sudden – changes.

I've seen many leaders give "speeches." They talk about the next quarter or the next year. It is a well-prepared speech. It makes a whole lot of sense, and it leads the audience by the hands to the expected outcome. It follows the often-used model of: *"I'm going to tell you X. I am telling you X. What I just told you was X."* Since there are no absurdities, paradoxes, or emotions, no one will remember what was said, nor how that made them feel.

To be able to "get out of tune," you need to be in tune. I'm not talking about speaking over a soft piece of jazz music (although you certainly could do that, and it might even help the audience remember even better[89]). No, I'm talking about an internal tune that starts to softly jive before you start to speak.

As a metronome, it guides your speaking pattern so you do not speak too fast. To some, it's enough just to imagine your fingers snapping in a given rhythm. Others have an internal "track" that starts playing. As you start to speak, you now have a rhythm that engages the audience the same way a song does. That is, your speech will be remembered by the implicit memory, just like that last song you heard on the radio this morning has been stuck in your head all day. You don't have to resort to actual absurdities to make a speech memorable. Just need to interrupt the tune for a moment – take an unexpected pause for a beat.

Talking to an implicit tune creates a pattern to your speaking, and as we have established, humans are hardwired to recognize patterns as a means of survival. When experiencing such a pattern, the brain releases dopamine to reward us[90]. That is how we learn to do the right things. We also get dopamine when we eat, or reproduce, to reinforce biological necessities positively. When we listen to a tune – implicit or explicit – we use additional parts of the brain to those used when just listening to speech[91]. This makes what you say more memorable.

Sometimes, it helps to simplify this advice a bit. I have often told people to imagine their words as written down and then sprinkle commas around haphazardly. Instead of saying:

"It is my absolute pleasure to present to you the utterly astonishing hostess of tonight:" say,

"It is, my absolute, pleasure to present to you, the, utterly, astonishing hostess, of tonight:"

Read the last sentence, but pause at the misplaced commas. Make a gesture with your hands as you do, making it a purposeful action.

Use the pauses – also the pauses that shouldn't be there. And use the words – the words that have a "distance" to the words people expect. A "distance" in psycholinguistics can be orthographic, phonological, or semantic. Use "porridge" instead of "oatmeal" or say "It takes two to... polka" instead of the expected "two to tango."

"But, I have to speak fast to get my points across. I don't even understand what psycholinguistic means!" someone once told me. And while the last point was fair – I tend to use very information-dense words almost to the point of sounding much too archaic and academic – the first point is a fallacy. An excellent speaker has rapport with the receiver(s) and will modulate the speed to match the comprehension level of the receiver.

I can almost hear the same person objecting: *"That's more of your psycho-babble linguistics – we all know that some languages are inherently spoken faster (like Spanish or Japanese) while some are slow and drag out the vowels (like Thai or Vietnamese)."* While that is true, those languages have different information densities per word, and the actual information rate is consistent.

To be precise, with a few exceptions, almost all languages transmit knowledge at 39 bits/s, according to a study by Coupé et al[92].

Let's take a break and show you a trick you can do completely with your voice. You are going to demonstrate how you can influence the audience using nothing but words. Carefully constructed words, but still just words.

I WANT TO BREAK FREE

A magic effect demonstrating that free will is but

AN ILLUSION

Imagine this. A spectator gets three choices. Before making the choices, you inform the spectator that you will influence them with your words and that the spectator should try to break free from your shenanigans.

You show your business card and tell the spectator that on the back side of the business card is the outcome of choices yet to be made.

IT IS A MANUSCRIPT OF THINGS TO COME THAT HAVE NOT YET HAPPENED.

The spectator makes three free choices, and you even ask if they want to change their mind. When the spectator is satisfied that the choices were indeed completely free, you turn over the manuscript which matches 100%, demonstrating that there is no such thing as free will. It is inspired by "Free Will" by magician Deddy Corbuzier.

You will need three random items. Let's assume they are: a credit card, a ring, and a key.

If you want to perform this, you can use any three items – they can even be borrowed. All you need to do is write the prediction to match the items. If you know the items beforehand, you can have the prediction already written.

You introduce your business card (or simply a folded piece of paper) and say:

"I have written something down on the back of my business card. It is a manuscript that describes actions that haven't taken place. Yet. In a moment, I want you to make three choices. Don't think too hard or too long about them. This demonstration aims to illustrate free will, and we all know what overthinking does to free will. So relax, and make your choices quickly and freely."

You introduce the three objects. They can be borrowed from the spectators.

The spectator is invited to put one of the objects into the pocket while the other two objects are distributed amongst you. One for the spectator, one for you. The exact wording will be shared in the method section, but the spectator decides who gets to have which object.

After the spectator has made the choices, you say: *"Remember the manuscript? Please turn it over and read what it says."*

The spectator turns over the business card which correctly predicts who has which items and what item is in the pocket.

This is a rare effect in terms of methodology because there is no secret "trick within the trick". The method is exactly what it seems. You are using clever wordings to achieve the desired illusion.

Because the secret is all in the words you use, it is somewhat difficult to teach because you will change directions depending on what the spectator says. We will go through all possible scenarios, which at first will seem overwhelming. It is like describing how to get from A to B during road work, and you don't know which roads will be closed, so you need to explain different routes simultaneously.

METHOD:

On the back of your business card, you have written a prediction like this:

I HAVE THE RING · YOU HAVE THE KEY · THE CREDIT CARD IS IN THE POCKET

This does not in and of itself raise any suspicions, but there are a few secrets of terrifying beauty in this. First of all, there really is only one prediction, and it is in full view all the time. You are not switching the prediction based on the spectator's choices.

The first thing we need to do is to ensure that the credit card ends up in the pocket. I will expose a method here that is near and dear to a lot of magicians, for good reasons. It is quite powerful. I don't believe I break the magician's code describing an effect using this method for a few reasons. First and foremost, the secret has its own Wikipedia page and is, therefore, already publicly available. Secondly, I believe that if the reader has read this far, enough intent has been shown that it is within the unwritten rules of magic that I can describe the secret.

Okay then, let's describe how the spectator freely chooses to put the credit card in the pocket.

The items are laid out as follows, from the view of the spectator, from left to right: Key, ring, credit card.

"Please place your right hand on one of the objects," you instruct the spectator.

People are inherently lazy, and since it apparently does not matter which object is chosen, most spectators will place their right hand on the credit card. If that happens, you continue: *"Excellent. Please put the object in your pocket."*

If the spectator does not select the credit card, you continue, without pausing a beat: *"and place your left hand on one of the other objects."*

Since this trick is based on words, it is important not to hesitate. The more naturally you speak, as if what happens is precisely as you expected, the better the effect.

If the situation is that the credit card is the remaining object, not covered by the spectator's hands, you say: *"Excellent choice of objects. I will place the remaining object in my pocket."*

The only situation we haven't covered is if the spectator chooses the credit card as object number two. If that happens, you continue: *"Excellent choice of objects, now hand one of them to me".*

If you are handed the credit card, you absent-mindedly place it in your pocket with a *"Great. I will put that in my pocket"* and begin the phase with the two remaining objects, which we haven't talked about yet. If the spectator is left with the credit card, you say, *"Excellent choice. Please place that in your pocket."*

What we have just been through has been a crash course in one of the strongest methods of mentalism.

THE EQUIVOQUE

Doing an equivoque is usually done with two objects. Doing it with three is quite advanced, and I apologize if this has been a difficult read. You have been exposed to an advanced utilization of the equivoque, and your mastery of this will earn you the respect of even knowledgeable magicians.

We have ensured that the credit card ends up in either your or the spectator's pocket. If you take a look back at the prediction, it does not say whose pocket it is in. It just says "in the pocket," meaning that any outcome will be covered.

We have gone through all the scenarios here, even the less likely ones, as you need to be prepared for all of them. The easiest are the ones where the credit card is selected as the first item or not at all. Luckily, these are also the scenarios with the highest probability.

Regardless of which choices were made, what is left is to distribute the two remaining objects between you and the spectator.

"Please hand me one of the objects and keep the other one to yourself", you say, *"and don't let me influence you in any way"*. The last sentence will probably make you smile from within because you are, at this point, done with all the influencing. The rest is showmanship.

"You have handed me the ring. Was that a free choice? If you feel it was not, I will give you the option to change your mind. Do you want to change your mind?"

As we shall see in a moment, it does not matter who ends up with the remaining two objects, so you can milk this for all it's worth, offering the spectator the chance to change minds a couple of times if need be.

Now, at some point, the spectator is happy with the choices, and there are now two possibilities.

Either you have the ring, or the spectator has the ring. The credit card will be in a pocket – either yours or the spectators.

This is your cue to determine who gets to read the prediction.

Assume the spectator has the ring. You say: *"Remember that this is a manuscript?"* as you point to the face down business card. *"Please turn it over and read it."* There is nothing odd about the spectator reading a manuscript, which is why we name it as such instead of a prediction.

The spectator will read the prediction and will be 100% correct.

The other option is that you have the ring. You say: *"Ok, so just to re-cap, you do not want to change your mind. This is the final choice. I have the ring, you have the key, and the business card is in the pocket? Let's see what the prediction says."*

You turn over the business card and read the prediction, which is 100% correct. I found that repeating the situation before reading the prediction greatly reinforces the effect. Seconds before, you were just describing an end state which could have been several, and now you are reading the exact same words.

The use of a triple equivoque has fooled laymen and magicians alike, and the more nonchalantly you deliver the script, the better the method is hidden.

To recap, the prediction is written, so it doesn't matter who has the ring and who has the key. You just switch who reads it.

The "forcing" of the credit card is done using the equivoque and will, if spoken without hesitation, seem like a completely free choice.

Since this trick packs small and plays big, it is the one I perform when I all of a sudden find myself in a situation where a trick would be good. Either to set the mood or just to answer, "Oh, you're a mentalist? Show us a trick". The trick is "impromptu", which means it can be done on the spot without any preperation.

I once performed this at a restaurant in Paris, France. It was before my time at the LEGO Group, and I was meeting the leadership team of one of our biggest customers. I was there with our CEO and the VP of Sales. Both extrovert and charming, having no problem interacting with the French leadership team. I, however, found I was struggling a bit. I had the advantage of speaking French, but since my colleagues did not, that did not help me. I decided to let them know that I was not just a senior leader, I also performed mentalism. This caught their interest, and they inquired if I would show them an example of mentalism. I chose this trick. I borrowed three items and wrote the prediction on the back of my business card.

I asked the customer's CEO to place his hand over the manuscript to ensure no one was meddling with it. I asked the COO (Chief Operating Officer) if she wanted to experience the sensation of magic. She would be delighted, and when I asked her to place her right hand on one of the objects, she went for the key.

"Excellent choice. As COO, you know that the key to the business is worth more than the credit card. Please place your other hand on an item". She placed her left hand on the ring. *"Great choices. As we all know, a ring can symbolize commitment, like a marriage or an engagement. Since we have a strong relationship, I knew you would pick that. That leaves the credit card, which I will place in my pocket."*

I paused, allowing for smiles and comments, before continuing: *"Now, please hand me either of the objects. It can be the one under your right hand or the one under your left. The choice is yours, but I am already now telling you that I know what you will pick, and I wrote it down on the back of the business card, which no one has touched but you?"* I said, looking at the CEO who confirmed with a laugh that he had been guarding it fiercely.

The COO handed me the key. *"Now are you sure that was a free choice? Maybe I influenced you with my comment before? Do you want to change your mind?"*. She declined and said she did not want to change her mind. *"I knew you wouldn't. But in a moment, you'd wish you had"*, I said with a smile. *"Now, can you please tell us all what the situation is? What is the outcome of your choices?"* I said, and she smilingly said: *"Well, I have the ring, you have the key, and the credit card is in your pocket. There is NO way you could have known that."*

I asked her to read the prediction, which was almost word for word what she had just said.

The rest of the evening went well. They even discussed which of them should have my business card with the prediction on it. The CEO was on Twitter[3], and I started following him, mostly as a courtesy.

Years passed, and I had forgotten all about this. I was now working for the LEGO Group but still following the CEO's Twitter account. One day I read a tweet from the CEO: *"Ten years ago, I witnessed the purest example of magic I have ever seen. I would love to know how to do this to delight my friends. Somehow, the magician could predict three completely free choices!"*. The trick had definitely made an impact on him as a person. Maybe also strengthened our business relationship, although I have no way of validating that, other than they remained customers for a long time.

The trick was done entirely with words. Both spoken words and some cleverly written words. None of these words came easy – it took many months to craft the trick so that it would pack a wallop.

In the next chapter, it makes sense then to take a step further into the world of rhetorical devices.

[3]Now X.com

WORDS DON'T COME EASY

The tools of the trade you didn't know you knew but want

TO KNOW NOW

LANGUAGE REVOLUTIONIZES. When humans developed the ability to speak, our cognitive abilities, such as memory, reasoning, and problem-solving skills, increased. With language came collaboration, and soon humans became the apex predator.

In the early 2020s, language revolutionized once again. AI development had been fragmented into distinct areas, making progress slow because progress was incremental per area, not the entire field. Then came a new interface – chat – and suddenly, language united the AI field, and we saw a huge spike in AI beginning in 2022.

What we are describing in this book is not a revolution. It is the natural evolution of language, to which most of us haven't been giving a second thought. Until now.

Let's look at how to make our words have a lasting impact.

"ASK NOT WHAT YOUR COUNTRY CAN DO FOR YOU, BUT WHAT YOU CAN DO FOR YOUR COUNTRY".

Most readers will not only remember that line but will also recognize it and maybe even be able to picture the clip from Kennedy's inaugural speech where he said those famous words.

But did you know that he was using a rhetorical device known as an **antimetabole?** This is a technique in which a phrase or sentence is

202

repeated but in reverse order, specifically used to create a memorable sentence. Most readers will probably remember, *"When the going gets tough, the tough get going"* which is an example of the same device.

We are going to spend a chapter on rhetorical devices. You probably do not know they are constructs, but you will have felt their impact.

Even if you are not a *Star Wars™* fan, you probably recognize this quote from Yoda: *"Fear leads to anger. Anger leads to hate. Hate leads to suffering"*. Yoda uses a clever little device called **anadiplosis**, in which a word or phrase at the end of one clause or sentence is repeated at the beginning of the next clause or sentence.

A similar construct was used in the olden days when you couldn't broadcast the news as you can today and relied on a phrase that was easy to convey. *"The king is dead. Long live the king"*. A construct in which a word or phrase is repeated at the beginning and the end of a clause or sentence is called a **panalepsis**. They can be so powerful that they can even implant false memories. Abraham Lincoln is often quoted for this panalepsis: *"You can fool some of the people all of the time, and all of the people some of the time, but you cannot fool all of the people all of the time"*, which he famously never said.

More than 2000 years ago, Caesar used a device called **asyndeton**. It is a rhetorical device in which conjunctions (such as "and," "or," or "but") are omitted from a series of words, phrases, or clauses. "I came, I saw, I conquered" or, in Latin, **"Veni, vidi, vici"**.

In a previous chapter, we discussed how to implant false memories and give unconscious commands using aspects of spoken words. But the chapter focused on how and what to do, not so much on why this works and where it comes from.

The examples that follow are just that – examples. That is, they do not necessarily represent facts. For instance, we begin where we ended the previous chapter – on the study of rhythmic speaking. We will use Shakespeare as an example because his writing uses several of the techniques that will be taught. But Shakespeare, to my knowledge, did not give any specific performance directions (beyond the famous "exit, pursued by a bear"). Therefore, I can't know for sure that his use of rhythm in writing was ever intended to be about performance – it might just have been to aid in reading the material and immersing into the story. Yet, Shakespeare's language capabilities are so profound that he makes a great study, regardless of his intentions at the time of writing.

The word used to describe the study of speech's rhythm, stress, and intonation is called **prosody**. In linguistics, prosody is the aspect of language that includes variations in pitch, loudness, speech tempo, and the use of the voice to convey meaning. Prosody is an essential aspect of language because it can help convey meaning, emphasis, and emotion and can play a role in understanding and interpreting spoken language. For example, a speaker's prosody can signal whether a sentence is a question or a statement or whether a word is stressed or unstressed.

William Shakespeare might have used prosody to regulate our attention and to make his work easy to recite and remember. We can't know his intentions, but he is known for his skillful use of prosody in his plays and poems. In Shakespeare's works, prosody is used to convey meaning, emphasis, and emotion and maybe also to create a rhythmic pattern that adds to the overall effect of the language.

For example, Shakespeare often uses iambic meter in his plays, which creates a regular pattern of unstressed and stressed syllables. An iamb is a metrical foot in poetry that consists of two syllables. The first being unstressed and the second being stressed. The word "iamb" itself is an example of an iamb. Iambs are one of the most common metrical feet in English poetry and are often used to create a regular rhythmic pattern known as the iambic meter. For example, the opening line of William Shakespeare's play Romeo and Juliet – "*Two households, both alike in dignity*" – is written in iambic pentameter, which means that it has five iambs per line. This creates a rhythmic pattern of unstressed-stressed syllables, giving the line a natural and flowing rhythm. This helps to convey the natural rhythm of speech and gives the lines a flowing and musical quality.

Sometimes, for additional effect, Shakespeare used the **trochee**, another metrical foot in poetry that consists of two syllables, with the first syllable stressed and the second syllable unstressed. The word "trochee" itself is an example of a trochee, with the first syllable "tro" being stressed and the second syllable "chee" being unstressed. Shakespeare used the trochee relatively infrequently in his works, but it was often for a specific effect when he did use it. For example, he might use a trochee to create a sense of speed or urgency or to add emphasis to a particular word or idea. He might also use the trochee to create a sense of contrast or tension by placing it in a line that is otherwise written in a different metric pattern.

Shakespeare's use of the trochee adds variety and complexity to his language and helps to create a unique and distinctive rhythm in his works. He uses it actively to break the rhythm that the audience is getting into, interrupting their cognitive reception pattern.

Another example would be Gertrude Stein. Her writing style was a departure from traditional literary forms and conventions, and she is considered one of the significant figures of the modernist movement. Stein's writing often emphasized the musicality of language, as she sought to create a rhythm that would shape the reader's experience of the text. She used repetition, alliteration, and other prosodic techniques to achieve this. Unfortunately, her writing is relatively unknown outside a narrow circle of literary and academic circles, even though she greatly inspired Ernest Hemmingway, F. Scott Fitzgerald, T.S. Elliott, and other members of The Lost Generation.

Her writing was heavily influenced by her interest in contemporary modernist art and her training in psychology, which emphasized the role of repetition in shaping the reader's emotional response. In her work, Stein sought to challenge conventional narrative structures and instead focus on the sounds and rhythms of words. This often resulted in a fragmented, nonlinear writing style, where the emphasis was placed on individual words and phrases rather than on a coherent narrative.

We see this effect in speaking, for instance, in Martin Luther King Jr.'s "I Have a Dream" speech. King uses rhythmic repetition and parallelism in this speech to create a powerful and compelling argument for racial equality. For example, he repeats the phrase "I have a dream" throughout the speech, using variations in pitch and emphasis to convey different emotions and ideas. This repetition helps create a strong and memorable rhythm that captures the audience's attention and reinforces the speech's main points. Additionally, King uses **parallelism** – the repetition of similar grammatical structures – to create a sense of unity and coherence in his argument. For example, he repeats "Let freedom ring" several times and uses similar phrasing in other parts of the speech to create a sense of unity and momentum.

Another example is former President Barack Obama's "Yes We Can" speech. In this speech, Obama uses variations in pitch, loudness, and tempo to convey different emotions and ideas. For example, he speaks more slowly and loudly when emphasizing key points and more quickly and quietly when conveying a sense of urgency or excitement. Additionally, Obama uses pauses and silence to create suspense and emphasis and give the audience time to process his words. Obama's use of prosody helps to make his speech more engaging and persuasive and helps to reinforce the main points he is trying to make. There's more interesting information should you be interested in learning more in "How the voice persuades[93]" by Zant & Berger.

The use of stimuli that are not words to modify the meaning of spoken language is called **Paralanguage**[94]. Paralanguage is the non-verbal aspect of communication that accompanies and modifies the meaning of spoken language. It includes factors such as tone of voice, pitch, loudness, tempo, intonation, facial expressions, gestures, and body language. Paralanguage can convey a wide range of meanings and emotions and play a crucial role in interpreting and understanding spoken language. For example, a speaker's tone of voice can indicate whether they are asking a question or making a statement or whether they are happy, sad, or angry. A speaker's facial expressions and gestures can also convey important information, such as whether they are bored, interested, or annoyed. Paralanguage is an important part of communication and can help to convey meaning and emotion in ways that words alone cannot.

There are other techniques in the same family as the above. The usage of these will fly by even knowledgeable people, as they are pretty obscure. They will achieve different outcomes, but now that we've opened the door to rhetoric, let's cover a few more techniques that are not that well-known.

Now, the first of the lesser-known techniques is **asterismos**, and I just used it in this sentence. It is when you use a word or a short phrase to call for the audience's attention at the beginning. It could be as simple as starting with "listen" or "now". An even lesser-known technique is **metonymy**, which is a metaphor that's not a metaphor and thus will require imagination from the audience. When using a metaphor, you want to transfer the qualities of one object to another, making it easier to understand. *"Her eyes shone like diamonds"* is a metaphor because the association and qualities of a diamond are positive. When using a metonymy, it is just about the description without any of the qualities. Like calling journalism "the press". We do that all the time – *"The press was invited to the event"* is a perfectly understandable sentence, even if the distance between journalists and the press is long, linguistically speaking. Porcelain is often called china due to its origins and is another example of metonymy. A deliberately placed metonymy in your sentence can make it as strong as a Long Island Ice tea served at an accounting convention. We can't say how strong because comparing techniques is like comparing apples to rabbits.

We live in a time where information and stimuli are everywhere, and sometimes it can be more impactful to use poor language than rich language in terms of meaning.

I don't know if I can explain the next concept in a way that makes it usable, but I will try. **Aporia** is something you've witnessed a lot if you watch any kind of performance art. When the tightrope walker in the circus pretends almost to fall, it is a feint to introduce doubt in the eyes of the audience. The more they think the artist could, in fact, fall, the more exciting they perceive the act. As you may have already guessed, I used aporia to begin this paragraph. I expressed doubt in my ability to explain it, but just like the artist in the circus, that was all a ploy to get your attention.

I am a big fan of transformational learning. That is, you can learn something in one domain and transfer that knowledge into another domain. You have witnessed it a lot on these pages, as examples and metaphors have been used to explain different ideas or methodologies. A benefit of this is that you can explain the same thing twice without repeating yourself. If you use different metaphors or examples, the repetition aids understanding.

The use of subtle repetition is called **exergasia** and is a rhetorical technique to bring forth a powerful idea. A fine example of exergasia is Winston Churchill's *"We Shall Fight on the Beaches"* speech. One of the main methods he used throughout the speech was the repetition of key phrases and ideas to emphasize and reinforce his main points. For example, he repeated the phrase *"we shall fight"* several times, using variations in emphasis and tone to convey a sense of determination and resolve. Churchill also used parallelism, in which he repeated similar grammatical structures to create a sense of coherence and unity in his argument. For example, he used parallel phrases such as *"we shall fight on the seas and oceans"* and *"we shall fight in the air"* to create a sense of momentum and to build towards his main point. The use of the same word to start each phrase – *"we shall"* – is known as **anaphora**. Anaphora is not only used to create compelling messages but messages that are easier to remember.

What I'm teaching you here is a communicative weapon of mass destruction. You will be able to slay your opponents and win every battle. And just to be clear, I wrote this primarily to introduce the next technique called **dysphemism**. A dysphemism in rhetoric is a method of giving your sentence an, often humorous, texture by replacing a neutral term with a negative one. It is the opposite of euphemism. In the example above, I used a couple of negative terms like "weapons of mass destruction," "slay your enemies" and "battle". You probably noticed it immediately because it is unlike the language I use myself, or indeed have used anywhere else in this book.

In the same ballpark, we find **litotes**, which is when you use a deliberate understatement as something positive, often using a double negative. In Danish, this is widely used. Especially in Jutland, where I live, saying *"det er ik' så ringe endda"* (it's not too bad) is said in praise of something that's really good. In English it's sometimes found in slang such as "not too shabby" or in constellations such as "well, it's not the *worst* meal I've ever had." If I have to say so myself, it was not the worst example in this chapter.

About 20% work harder after a charismatic speech, and approximately 20% give more to charity than people who listened to a non-charismatic speech[95].

While the theories of rhetorical shenanigans settle, I get the feeling that we have been spending a disproportionate amount of time talking about talking. But like you can't teach writing without teaching reading, you can't teach magical language without touching on magical reading. Or, as it is known in the entertainment industry: mind reading.

THE
ACE
OF
SPADES

HOW TO
CREATE A CHORAL
HARMONY
of two stories told at the same time

Before we talk about mind reading, it is perhaps appropriate to remind ourselves where we are coming from—the magic world of illusion where nothing is as it seems. At the beginning of the book, you are taught how to know who is secretly holding a LEGO brick. During the trick, you seemingly give away the method. In reality, the pseudo method you are revealing demonstrates much stronger abilities than the actual method, which is purely mathematical.

HERE'S ONE OF THE PROFOUND SECRETS OF MAGIC: IT IS NOT JUST IMPRESSIVE IN THE IMAGINARY WORLD BUT ALSO IN THE REAL WORLD.

This means that the audience might enjoy the illusion of what they are witnessing, but they are also impressed by the skills that the magician ostensibly possesses to pull off the trick. It is an extra layer of entertainment that separates magic from many other performance arts. The audience might be impressed by a juggler or someone who can memorize a phone book, but they are only impressed by the performer's skills. There is no illusion, no suspension of disbelief.

The reactions you achieve as a magician comes from the former just as much as the latter. You are demonstrating a beautiful illusion (that is not really happening; it just appears so) using amazing skills (that you don't really have, it just appears so).

The "real" magic, so to speak, occurs when these two are mixed into one performance. It is the sorcerer's stone—the secret ingredient. When you see a bad magician, it is often because they are just using one of the two parts. You will see highly skilled individuals doing amazing feats with cards that are indistinguishable from juggling. Or you will see a pretentious mind reader using fancy words, but no real illusion is taking place.

This is the real secret of good magic. You are telling two stories at once, doubling the impact.

Think about that for a moment. What are some examples in your life where you could double your impact by telling two stories simultaneously?

GOOD PERFORMERS TELL A STORY. GREAT PERFORMERS TELL TWO PARALLEL STORIES.

When the leader presents the ambitious story of a bold yet achievable vision and combines it with a story of the capabilities, processes, and skills that will be built to achieve it. It is a combination of something we imagine (the bold vision) and something we do (prepare the organization to execute the vision).

The entrepreneur looking for venture capital is a sorcerer, weaving an enchanting tale of vision and possibility while demonstrating a resolute dedication to the craft. The entrepreneur describes the imaginary story of inspired innovations along with a dedication to building prototypes, testing assumptions, and problem-solving challenges, fostering optimism with a dash of realism. They cast a sprawling, imaginative story of innovation and opportunity, painting vibrant pictures of a dazzling future barely out of reach. And yet, beneath this magic, a strong and steady current of compounded competence runs.

Imagination takes flesh when vision and skill combine, and the improbable becomes provable. Stories intertwine to weave a fabric both fantastical and forge-worthy, tactical as much as tactile. Audiences may gasp at wonders almost too wild to credit yet find themselves admiring not mad folly but rather the sly sorcery of it all.

LET'S MAKE THIS REAL.

I will teach you a trick that is easy to do but has a significant impact. You can present this as a feat of mind control or fantastic sleight of hand, yet it uses neither to accomplish the effect. All that is required is that you and your spectators are familiar with poker rules.

You will show a card trick where you continue to win in poker, even if the spectator seemingly controls more and more of the actions. You will tell a story of how you influence the spectator's behavior, who is unaware of how you control their actions.

The trick presented here is, once again, inspired by something shown to me by magician Harry Lorayne. First, we will describe what the spectators see. Then, I will teach you the secret.

ARE YOU EXCITED YET?

"I will do a simple yet effective demonstration of how magicians can cheat at poker. We will just use two poker hands to make it as simple as possible."

As you say these words, you throw two times five cards on the table, face down. A poker hand is five cards, which means there are now a total of ten cards on the table.

You arrange the ten cards face down in a row between you and the spectator and say:

"We are going to take turns each selecting a face-down card like this. You are free to choose whichever card you want".

When each of you has five cards, you proceed by saying:

"Notice that you had a free choice of every card, yet I still won the hand. Let's turn the cards face up and see."

You each turn the cards face up, and you are indeed the winner with the best hand.

"Let's do it again, this time making it even fairer to you", you say.

This time, as you spread the ten cards out in the row, you turn some of them face up.

"As before, we each take turns taking a card like this. At each turn, you will decide if I should take a face-up or face-down card. When it is your turn, you have a free choice of a face-up or face-down card. I will try to influence your choice of cards. Try not to let me do that. Decide early on which cards you want; even if you get an unexplainable urge to change your mind, try not to do so. Or, if you do change your mind, change it twice."

As before, you each take turns taking cards. If the spectator tells you to take a face-up card, you do that. If they tell you to take a face-down card, you comply.

"Now, as you picked your cards, did you manage to resist my influence?"

You might smile at this sentence because, by now, you understand what is going on here linguistically. It doesn't matter if the spectator answers "yes" or "no" to that question. Either answer will build the scenario that you are indeed controlling the actions. If the spectator says "yes", it presupposes the existence of influence – otherwise, there would be nothing to resist. If the spectator says "no", not only does it presupposes the controlling, it also demonstrates that the spectator could not resist. We are telling a story of amazing abilities while doing the trick.

"Now, let's do this a third and final time, this time giving you more advantages. Please pick up the cards. Shuffle them thoroughly, and you deal all the cards. I am not touching the cards; all I can do to win this game is through my magical influence. To make this even fairer, before I look at my cards, you take a look at your cards and switch out your weakest card for one of mine."

The spectator picks up the cards, shuffles them, and deals all the cards into two hands of five cards.

"Now, as a final demonstration of nonverbal behavior control. Even if you made all the choices. And I do want to stress that you made all the choices, I still got the winning hand."

As you say that, each of you shows your hands, and lo and behold, you are again the winner.

Can you imagine how amazed the spectator is? Even with all the visible control given to the spectator, you seem to possess some kind of invisible control.

What the audience saw was a magic trick where you win each hand. Without the narrative, this is but a puzzle. A juggling trick. The magic happens when they discover how you control their choices, and they try to counter the manipulation.

As with most magic effects, the secret is the narrative. The method that makes you win is quite simple. Don't let the simplicity stop you from trying this out. It is a classic for a reason. It has amazed audiences for many years.

The ten cards are comprised of three times three of a kind. You might have 3 eights, 3 queens and 3 aces. That leaves one card, which can be any card, as long as it is not an eight, queen or ace, because that would allow for someone to have four of a kind. This "odd one out" card we call the Jonah card. You could just run through the deck of cards, picking out 3 batches of 3 of a kind, but that might make it too obvious. A better idea is to pre-arrange the stack on top of the deck. To avoid counting, you can have the 9 cards and then the Jonah card. It is then easy to pick the 10 cards because you take every card from, including the Jonah card.

This last card was named the "Jonah card" when it was first described in 1947[96]. The secret to this trick is, that whoever gets the Jonah card will lose. Your mission, should you choose to accept it, is to make sure the opponent gets the Jonah card at each turn. Let's see how to accomplish that:

You are going to mark the Jonah card. The best way to mark it is to use a sharp knife to scratch out some of the decoration on the back of the card. You will scratch an X in the card's top left and bottom right corners.

Here is an example using the back side design of my favorite brand of playing cards, Bicycle[4]. The top card is marked with a subtle scratched-out X. Notice that it is marked twice, so you can see it even if the card is rotated.

If you know how to control a card using sleight of hand, a marked card is not strictly necessary. However, it makes the method easy and allows you to focus on the narrative.

---

[4]Card aficionado will notice it is not 100% Bicycle brand.
 The card was generated by AI.

Marked cards have been used since probably five minutes after people started playing cards. When you read this, you might think, "That's an obvious mark". Try to mark the card as instructed and show the 10 cards to friends or family without showing the trick. Ask them if they notice anything. If they do, the mark is not subtle enough. But, hear me out; a card marked with this method will fly by almost everyone.

With the card marked, you will now know how to avoid it.

PHASE 1: Our dear friend, math helps us here. As you say "like this" (look at the narrative part) you are taking the first card. As long as you do not pick the Jonah card, the spectator will end up having it. With an even number of cards, the spectator will have the last choice, so even if no one happens to pick the Jonah card, the specator will end up with it, and you will win.

PHASE 2: Notice in the patterline there is a "like this" again. You will pick the first card, avoiding the Jonah card. As you turn the cards face up, avoid turning over the Jonah card to limit the spectator's exposure to this odd-one-out card. If you happen to do so, it's not the end of the world, and you can continue the trick, but I prefer it to be face down. Now when you select your first card, just avoid the Jonah card and continue as before.

PHASE 3: This will throw off even those who know the trick. Since the spectator does all of the dealing, 50% of the time, you will end up with the Jonah card. We will deal with that momentarily, but just appreciate that 50% of the time, you can just lean back and be completely hands-off for a stunning miracle. Let's assume you do get the Jonah card. If you do, you say as was presented in the above patterline. Under the guise of "to make this fairer", you offer the spectator to exchange the weakest card with one of yours, even if you haven't seen your cards. You will push forward the marked card, the Jonah card, and exchange it for whichever card the spectator gives you.

There is a scenario where the spectator has a full house and does not want to change cards. If that happens, applaud the spectator for resisting your influence and discuss how that was accomplished. However, the probability for this to happen is less than 3%. I have never experienced it despite having performed this trick many times. However, the effect is just as strong should it happen.

You are now ready to do an amazing demonstration of magic or mentalism. You can present this as a feat of influence, or you might want to demonstrate that you stop time and switch the cards. The reality you build around the illusion is up to you.

What you are saying and the story you are conveying are two different things. The more you can activate the imagination in the mind of the person you are talking with, the better. The biggest stories emerge not from your mouth but in the mind of the listener.

Let's take a step into the mind of the listener.

I FEEL GOOD

The epistemology and ontology
of mind-reading and how to apply it

OUTSIDE ENTERTAINMENT

As the audiences I perform for rarely understand what a "mentalist" is, I am often introduced as a "mind reader." That label places some expectations on me, and I had to have at least a few effects on my repertoire that demonstrated mind reading.

To no surprise to anyone, mentalists can't actually read minds. We rely on methods from the magic arsenal to do one of two things. Either we use a psychological force to plant the word in the spectator's mind, only to pretend to read it moments later, or we use one of the countless methods from magic to obtain knowledge of a word or selection secretly. That is until the method fails and you're on stage in front of hundreds of people, having no idea of what the person is thinking. As the saying goes: "Necessity is the mother of invention", and some of my biggest applause came when I had to resort to "real" mind reading because my magical apparatus failed to provide me with vital information.

I remember a particular time when I was hired to perform again at the same venue – to different people but the same demographics. I had on my repertoire a part where a spectator was thinking of a word, and upon writing the word down, I had a secret method of obtaining what was written down. So, it wasn't a difficult trick, and I could spend all my energy pretending to read the word from the spectator's mind. As I already knew the word, I approached the spectator with a lot of confidence, and sometimes they would burst out in laughter, saying something like *"I know you know I'm thinking of a bicycle"*. This happened more than once, and it saved me that day on stage when I couldn't read what the spectator had written down. I approached her with the same confidence, clearly signaling that I knew what she was thinking, and sure enough, at some point, when I was staring her in the eyes using my "mentalist look", she laughed, *"you already know I'm thinking of a birthday cake, right?"*.

When I return to my day job as a leader, I bring the skills of a mind reader with me, but with the mindset of the bonus princeps. There are very few situations where you should use the skills to which you are about to be introduced. More often than not, your job as a leader is to be cautious enough not to read minds.

"Why are you so angry?" Sydney had asked Jordan in an attempt to help him, as she felt the group would accept him more if he weren't so angry.

Jordan was outraged by that comment. His eye surgery didn't go as planned, and not only did he have to squint to read, he had a thunderous headache that just didn't want to go away.

See, Jordan wasn't angry, but he sure looked like that. So much that Sidney made a "mind read." A mind read that was so convincing that she believed it herself. She didn't know if he was angry because she hadn't asked. But she believed it because she made an unconscious mind read. The consequence of her mindreading is that Jordan's state of mind has changed, and now he is angry.

You don't really know how anyone is feeling. Or what they were thinking. Even when people say, "I feel good", we don't know what they feel. We have a responsibility as leaders to avoid reading minds if possible. Everyday greetings like "How are you?" illustrate this point. Regardless of accuracy, the automatic "Fine" response shows how ingrained this mind-reading habit is in social interactions. But by becoming more conscious of these knee-jerk assumptions, leaders can break the cycle and model a more authentic way of communicating.

We should all try not to react to a mind-read, because that is all that it is. A mind-read. It can be real, and it can be imaginary, and the only way to know for sure is to ask questions. People tend to react negatively to a mind-read. The question *"Why are you mad?"* is more of an accusation than a question. *"Why don't you understand what I'm saying"* likewise. It assumes and accuses in the same sentence, and it's obviously not good communication.

We already saw one example of mind-read in the chapter about magical influence, where Ben thinks he is helping Joan. Ben's reactions towards Joan stem from "confirmation bias", which is the tendency to draw conclusions about a person based on your own desires and beliefs instead of objectively observing the other person. A mind read is sometimes based on confirmation bias and sometimes what is known as unconscious bias, which comes in different shapes and forms.

Unconscious bias is present from the moment we meet another person.

Try this thought experiment: The scene is a cocktail party celebrating the release of the new book "An unexpected leadership journey". Two of the invited people randomly meet and start talking. They do not know each other. What do they spend the first couple of minutes talking about? My guess (mind read) is that you imagined the conversation to be around things they have in common.

"So, how do you know the author – Christian?
Are you a leader or a magician?"

"Where are you from?"

"Where did you study?"

"Oh, so you might know James?"

"Oh, so you also like magic?"

When people meet, the affinity bias makes us look for similarities, and we tend to connect better with people with whom we share interests, experiences, connections, or backgrounds.

All of a sudden, people start to move towards the main hall. Our two guests are not sure why, but they follow the crowd. After all, everyone else is moving towards the main hall, so it makes sense to just do as the majority—another bias in action.

We all have these learned attitudes or stereotypes that make us do mind reads, make assumptions about people, and react to these assumptions.

Being aware of your unconscious bias and not reacting to a mind-read is an important part of being a leader. The paradox here is that using your bias and gut feeling is an essential tool if you are deliberately trying to do a mind-read. Gut feelings have been in our vocabulary much longer than the evidence for it. Some scholarly articles debate gut feelings[97], but for now, we just have to accept them as a mix of our bias and a summary of what we, consciously and subconsciously, have observed. Our biases are, in and of themselves, just a collection of fundamental beliefs[98].

Sometimes, reading minds can be a necessity, though. Granted, the situation happens more often if you are a mentalist, but there are situations where it can come in handy as a leader, therapist, or coach. For instance, if you are dealing with a person hindered by limiting beliefs.

Limiting beliefs are negative thoughts or beliefs about ourselves or the world that restrict our ability to achieve our goals or live fulfilling lives. They can be as generic as "I am not good enough" or "I am not talented enough to succeed" to very specific beliefs "I need to get a promotion at this company to be successful".

LIMITING BELIEFS ARE OFTEN IMAGINARY BECAUSE THEY CANNOT BE OBSERVED OR PROVED IN THE REAL WORLD.

They are imagined convictions that limit the person. We talked about illusion questions in a previous chapter. They are useful in bringing a person's state of mind into reality. Through the process, we discover limiting beliefs that were imaginary, and hopefully, the problems the person was facing are now lesser than before as those beliefs are removed through the described process.

But sometimes, the person you are dealing with is incapable of transcending from imagination to reality for various reasons.

Maybe the person is feeling only the effect of a problem or a limiting belief but is utterly unaware of what it is.

Or maybe the person has been through a traumatic event, and the lines have been blurred. Sometimes, we deal with people who are not putting enough words into the issue at hand. Sometimes on purpose, but often involuntarily. Sometimes, the only way to solve a problem is through mind reading. I trust that I have given sufficient evidence for being careful with this skill, and if you are in doubt, don't use it. With that caveat emptor, let us learn how to read minds.

As a mentalist, it is useful to learn some basic statistics. A person born in the 2010s is likelier to be called Emma, Noah, Liam, or Olivia than John, Mary, or Helen, which are typical names for someone older (depending on the country, of course). Some stats are public and can be learned, and some you will have to collect yourself. During my long tenure as a mentalist, I have found that if I ask a person to draw a simple drawing on a slip of paper, the woman draws a heart and the man a smiley face. Or, if not one of these, it's a car, a tree, a house, or a stick figure.

If you ask for someone to think of a tool and the color of that tool, it is usually a hammer and red. The most commonly used color in art is yellow, perhaps because yellow was the first color humans managed to create from naturally occurring yellow ochre.

As a leader or a coach, you probably don't have the luxury of being able to limit the outcome space like we can in entertainment. That is, you can't ask people to think within a confined space of outcomes as a mentalist can. Within entertainment, it makes sense to say, "Pick a card" or "Think of a star sign", but in real life, the outcome space of a thought is endless.

You start from scratch, which we will now explore.

The first thing you will do to read the other person is to know how they are feeling. Tread this road carefully because the way to know what they are feeling is actually to feel what they are feeling. To accomplish this, we use a technique called emotional embodiment or embodied cognition.

Imagine a person walking down the street. He is sad and unhappy. Life has given him some curveballs, and he's carrying the weight of bad choices on his shoulders.

Now imagine another person, same age, gender etc. This person is happy. He just got promoted, and his girlfriend accepted his proposal. He is on his way to tell his best friend.

Do you think you can guess who is who based on their posture?

It has long been known that our feelings impact our emotions and body. If we are happy, we smile. If we are sad, we cry. However, as mentioned earlier, we can also cry from happiness and laugh nervously. Either way, our feelings impact our bodies. For the past 50 years, scientists have been trying to figure out if this is a bilateral effect.

If you constantly have your head down low, will that make you sadder? If you smile, will that impact your emotions and make you happier? Recent studies such as *"A multi-lab test of the facial feedback hypothesis by the Many Smiles Collaboration[99]"* present overwhelming evidence supporting this hypothesis. This is quite a comprehensive study with 49 authors who go to great lengths to cover any pre-existing biases before collecting data.

THE BODY-TO-EMOTION PATH IS BIDIRECTIONAL.

Looking at our language, this has been known before it was proven. Ancient cultures long believed that emotions and illnesses are connected. They believed that certain bodily fluids, called the four humors (blood, yellow bile, black bile, and phlegm), were responsible for health and disease. They believed that imbalances in these fluids caused illnesses and were often caused by emotions. This belief is still reflected in our language today. The word "melancholy," for example, comes from Latin words meaning "black" and "bitter bile," and we describe someone as "melancholic" when they're feeling gloomy or bitter. Similarly, the word "phlegmatic" describes someone calm and not easily moved, which is believed to be caused by an excess of phlegm in the body.

The scientific idea that emotions are not just cognitive or mental experiences but also physical experiences linked to the body can be found in research from different disciplines, starting from William James' work[100] on the topic in the late 1800s. He argues that emotions are not just mental states but are also experienced in the body.

Emotions are embodied in the physiological changes that occur in the body, such as changes in heart rate, breathing, muscle tension, and other physiological responses. When we experience an emotion, it activates a cascade of physiological changes in the body. For example, when we feel fear, our heart rate increases, we may start to sweat, and our muscles may tense up.

Similarly, when we feel happy, our heart rate may decrease, our breathing may become more relaxed, and we may feel a sense of warmth in our chest. These changes in the body can influence our cognitive and emotional experiences, and this bidirectional relationship between emotions, body, and cognition is a key point. Emotions can be conveyed through body language and perceived by others through nonverbal cues, such as facial expressions and posture.

The work on emotional embodiment includes the Somatic marker hypothesis[101], which argues that emotions and the body are closely connected. According to this hypothesis, our body generates an emotional response when we encounter an emotionally significant stimulus, such as a potential danger or a rewarding opportunity. These emotional responses, known as somatic markers, are then stored in the brain as patterns of neural activity. These markers are then used to guide future decisions by signaling the potential outcomes of different actions. Emotions are not isolated from other cognitive processes such as attention, perception, memory, reasoning, and decision-making. Emotions and feelings play a critical role in shaping processes by organizing the information to highlight the most meaningful or relevant aspects of the situation.

Some theories suggest that our consciousness is not stored in, nor confined to, the brain. The Extended Mind Theory[102] says that the mind is not just a product of the brain but is a product of a dynamic interaction between the brain, the body, and the environment. The tools and technologies that we use, such as smartphones, become an extension of our mind, and thus consciousness extends beyond the brain and into these tools. The body is not just a passive vessel that houses the mind but actively shapes and constructs our experiences, including our thoughts and perceptions. The theory challenges the traditional view of consciousness as being located solely within the brain.

Examples of this theory

REFLEXES: Our bodies have automatic reflexes that respond to certain stimuli without conscious thought. For example, if we touch a hot stove, our hand automatically withdraws before we have a chance to process the information consciously. This shows that our bodies can make decisions without the brain's involvement.

EMOTIONAL RESPONSES: Emotions are often experienced as physical sensations in the body, such as a racing heart or sweating palms. These emotional responses can influence our behavior and decision-making even if we are not consciously aware of them. For example, when we feel afraid, our bodies may respond by preparing us to fight or flee before our brains have had a chance to process the information.

HABIT FORMATION: Habits can be formed as a result of repeated actions and experiences, and once established, they can be performed automatically without conscious thought. For example, when we learn to ride a bike, we initially need to consciously think about every step involved. Over time, however, the process becomes automatic, and our bodies are able to perform it without the need for conscious thought.

The scientific studies of cognitive embodiment continue to bring up interesting facts. When we are in love, we get fewer colds[103]. This is a direct consequence of how a feeling impacts the body.

The body and our emotions are closely interlinked, and we can use this property to read another person's feelings.

YOU CAN FEEL WHAT THE OTHER PERSON IS FEELING IF YOU DELIBERATELY MIRROR EVERYTHING ABOUT THEIR PRESENCE AND PAY CLOSE ATTENTION TO CHANGES IN YOUR OWN MOOD.

I have to repeat that this can be dangerous – you don't know how bad the other person's mental state is. While you will not feel it equally, it will impact you. Emotional contagion happens subconsciously but can be harnessed and used to learn how someone feels. Since it entails mimicking the other person's physical appearance, we can call the method mirroring.

Learning how to mirror another person is not easy, and you will need someone to practice with.

Find a suitable practicing partner and begin by facing each other. Standing or sitting. You try to match the other person as closely as possible. Then, close your eyes while the other person shifts position. Open your eyes and try to match the other person. Now, repeat this process a few cycles, each time with a smaller and smaller change. It will eventually come down to a small facial expression or a minuscule shift in the head position. Continue until you can't figure out what changed and have to ask the other person what was moved. It will become a fun game where the other person will try to hide the changes for you, and you will try to match them anyway. Don't be discouraged if you can only do three or four cycles before giving up – the learning curve is not steep, and you will soon get a grasp of it.

Eventually, you will be able to match every aspect of the other person's posture, and due to the cognitive embodiment feedback, you will also start to feel what the other person is feeling. Be aware of the beforementioned affinity bias. This is the bias that we attract people who are like ourselves. I was once practicing this at a café, matching a woman sitting at another table. When she left, she stopped by my table and asked, *"I'm sorry, but surely we know each other from somewhere?"* I stopped practicing without consent after that episode, and you should always get consent and agreement before practicing matching someone else.

The (side) effect of gaining rapport with another person by mirroring has been explored in NLP[104] (Neuro Linguistic Programming). They combine this with matching, which matches other characteristics such as voice tonality, pitch, speed etc.

As you understand how the other person is feeling, it is time to get closer to what they are thinking. If you are already familiar with hypnosis, there is some transformational learning here because the process is not that different from what is known as induction in hypnosis - even if it has nothing at all to do with hypnosis. We are not hypnotizing anyone in the process.

When a hypnotist does an induction (establishing the conditions to enable hypnosis to occur), everything that happens is attributed to the subject getting into a trance. This aids the process. The subject might sigh, or maybe the arm drops to the side. Even if this is purely unrelated, the hypnotist will say something like: *"As you get further into a trance, you will feel the urge to sigh, and when your arm drops, you will drift further into a state of relaxation"*. This form of reframing, called utilization, makes the subject comfortable that everything is going as planned and that the induction is working. It works by creating positive interference – like gently pushing a swing. There is no resistance in the subject's mind, and you are aiming for a smooth transition into a trance.

Mind reading is along the same lines. You are removing any resistance from the subject indicating the nature of what is on their mind. You signal clearly that you already know, creating a smooth transition into knowing what the subject is thinking. The science of this is called the Theory of Mind, which originated with René Descartes[105] and evolved in the 1970s through the work of David Premack[106] and others[107]. A variety of people have independently proposed the connection to mind reading, but probably the first to write a substantial body of work on this was Simon Baron-Cohen[108]. He is also the inventor of the "Mind in the Eyes test", designed to assess the theory of mind abilities, or the ability to understand and interpret the mental states of others, such as beliefs, desires, intentions, and emotions.

It is important to note that the theory of mind does not involve the ability to read other people's thoughts. Rather, it involves the ability to infer what someone else might think or feel based on their behavior and the context in which they interact. We must take it a step further to get to the actual thought if that is what we are after.

We now see a significant difference between mind-reading as an entertainment piece, and mind-reading in a professional setting. As a mentalist, I get the biggest applause if I can tell the exact word or topic the spectator has in mind. As a professional, the specifics are not as important as the intent. This is probably a good thing because, as mentioned in the beginning, real mind reading is an illusion. In the realm of entertainment, we can create the illusion of real mind reading down to the specifics. What we are bringing with us from that realm are the methods to get an understanding of the subject's thoughts. Thoughts that most often are hidden not only from you but from the subject as well. It begins with utilizing the Forer Effect[109].

Forer was a psychologist, and he gave his students what they believed was an assessment of their personalities based on a test they had taken. They were asked to rate the accuracy of the assessment from 1-5, and the average turned out to be 4.30. That is pretty amazing, given that they had all received the same assessment, and the test results were not used. The effect continues to appear in psychological studies[110] but quickly became popular in the field of entertainment, including fortune tellers and mediums.

When used outside psychology, it is sometimes called The Barnum Effect after P.T. Barnum, the famous showman who excelled at using this and other methods to captivate his audience. It is part of a technique called **Cold Reading**, meaning that you read a person without prior knowledge – the person is "cold".

We use this in mind reading in direct continuation of the previous step. That is, we are making the subject comfortable with the fact that we know what they are thinking, lowering their defenses. These defenses can be deliberate or subconscious. Usually, when performing on stage as a mentalist, the subject will try to hide the word they are thinking of, as this is the "game" that the mentalist and the spectator play. Suppose you happen to find yourself in a professional situation where you need to read minds. In that case, the defense is usually subconscious, as the subject has no anticipation of having their mind read. Sometimes, a subject has a limiting belief. Something that is holding the person back from living their life or achieving their dreams. And sometimes, the person is not even aware of what that is. A mind read might, in some cases, help identify and eliminate that belief. Here are some examples of limiting beliefs:

"I'm not good enough."

"I'll never be able to achieve my goals."

"I'm not smart enough."

"I'm not attractive enough."

"I'm too old to change."

"I'm not capable of making my own decisions."

"I'm not worthy of love and happiness."

"I don't deserve success."

"I'll never be able to make enough money."

"I'm not strong enough to handle difficult situations."

Notice that a common trait of limiting beliefs is that they are impossible to quantify. They exist in the imaginary space, but their impact on a person is observable in the real space. What does "good enough" mean, how is it measured, and how do you know if you are good enough?

I once had an employee with a limiting belief holding her back. I noticed a position available that she was qualified for, and it would be a career move for her if she got it. Remember the example with Joan in the chapter on influence? Here, a leader was helping an employee get a promotion that she really didn't want. It was presented as an example of when you shouldn't use your influence because you don't know what the employee really wants.

Therefore, this story begins with understanding what the employee wanted and whether she was moving towards that goal. I quickly learned that she wanted to apply, but she did not do it because she felt she was not qualified.

This led to the first step – identifying the limiting belief. I found that she was convinced she wasn't good enough, but she had never considered that an imaginary belief. By identifying it, we can start challenging it. It is not unlike the "name it to tame it" wording Daniel Siegel popularized[111].

Following the flow of mind-reading, we are not judging the belief or saying that the person is wrong for believing it. We are simply enabling the person to see it from a different view. The belief may or may not be true, and we can use illusion questions to look for evidence that contradicts the belief. If we can find examples of situations where the person has succeeded, then that might count as evidence that "I am not good enough" is not true and maybe replace it with something that we know is true and that is more real than imaginary.

In this example, I was playing back the mind read with different wordings. I asked her if she was willing to replace *"I am not good enough"* with something like *"I am constantly learning, hungry for knowledge and improvement"*. Now this had the same flavor as the existing belief, but it is observable in the real world, and more importantly, it is not a limiting belief but an enabling belief.

There might also be situations where the person is deliberately holding something back.

I had just hired Bonnie. The hiring process had been long, as I had specific wishes for the role, and very few candidates fit all parameters. But Bonnie did, and not only was I satisfied with the hire, but I also made sure Bonnie knew how much I appreciated her joining the team and was looking forward to working with her.

One day, Bonnie came into my office and shut the door. She sat down and started asking a few mundane questions. I indulged her and engaged in the conversation, which seemed to go nowhere. I noticed she was clenching her fists to the point that her knuckles were turning white. I decided to see if he could help her achieve what she came to my office for with a mind-read.

"Listen, I know people are often uncomfortable being in the situation you're in", I began the read. I am not saying I knew what situation she was in, as I had no idea at the time. I could tell she was uncomfortable, and I could make the statement with and without knowing the details, using the Forer effect.

"I want you to know it's okay", I continued, noticing Bonnie's knuckles getting a more healthy color.

"Oh, I was so afraid to tell you. I almost threw up outside your office", she finally said.

"Why were you afraid? Have you experienced someone taking offense before?" I asked.

"Yes, when I resigned from my last job to join you, my boss was yelling at me, which was very uncomfortable. So I was petrified you would react the same way, as I haven't been here for a full month yet." Bonnie said.

She had gotten an offer from another company, so she was in my office to hand in her resignation. By doing a mind-read I shortened the time she had to feel uncomfortable. Bonnie got the impression that I knew already, and it made it easier for her to talk about it.

Using mind reading in leadership can, according to some studies, increase your authenticity[112]. It turns out that when people make decisions based on their intuition rather than deliberating, they feel more authentic and are also perceived as more authentic. Using the principles of mind-reading as a tool to increase intuition is a choice we can make, depending on the situation.

"Mind-reading" in the professional context is about being aware of your biases and trying to act objectively. It is about using sensory acuity to navigate with the flow for minimum resistance. We are trying to minimize the Hawthorne effect[113], which is the theory that people change behavior if they feel they are being observed, studied, or analyzed. The more natural the conversation, the more information is transferred.

Some of the scientific studies in this area are interesting because they mix magic with science. In the 2023 paper *"Emulating future neurotechnology using magic[114]"*, researchers utilize magic tricks as part of their experiments. The experiments took the Forer effect into the present time. The participants would face an advanced neuro-technical machine that could read their minds and was asked to assess the accuracy. 80% agreed that the (randomly generated) feedback was accurate and even provided rationalizations to support it. I like this study because the researchers integrated mentalism as part of it and proved a point we're using in this book.

I recognize that the connection between the magic and professional versions of mind-reading is probably more distinct than in the other chapters, where the utilization might be more apparent. I include this part anyway because mind-reading is such a big part of the mentalist role that the book would seem incomplete without it. And, by completing the repertoire, we can now start distilling this into a conclusion. In the next chapter, let's take a step back and look at it with fresh eyes.

SPACE ODDITY

The fifth element of

LEADERSHIP AND MAGIC

I have used the word **aether** frequently throughout this book. Historically, the word was used to explain, for instance, how light could travel through a vacuum. Also known as "the 5th element" or sometimes "quintessence," it was thought to be the medium that inhibited the empty space. The aether was primarily used as a metaphysical element, and the demise of the aether came, paradoxically, through the scientific acceptance of the aether.

Scientists such as Bernouilli, Huygen, and even Newton began to use aether to explain their theories. It is even present in Newton's description of gravity in "Philosophiæ Naturalis Principia Mathematica." From thereon, the aether slowly began to vanish from science and, in turn, philosophy and metaphysics as well. While that was a healthy move for physics – aether is not a real thing that can be measured or observed, I find the metaphorical aspect of aether appropriate to describe the quintessence of magic and leadership.

Stories can live for thousands of years. Before writing, stories lived by being told or as songs. They moved in time and space, and I find the aether to be the best analogy for where stories live.

MAGIC IS NOT THE MAGICIAN; IT IS THE INTERACTIONS THAT HAP-PEN BETWEEN PEOPLE.

YOUR ORGANIZATION IS NOT YOUR PEOPLE; IT IS THE RELATION-SHIPS AND INTERACTIONS BETWEEN THE EMPLOYEES.

LOVE IS NOT THE COUPLE; IT IS WHAT HAPPENS BETWEEN THEM.

Like Mozart famously never said: *"Music is not the individual notes; it is the pauses in between."*

When you look at the flock of birds flying over the treetops in the sunset, it is clear that the movement is not that of the individual bird; it is the movement of all the space between the birds. Even the flying bird itself is not the individual parts. Muscle, bones, beak, feather – none of that makes flying. If it did, ostriches and kiwis could fly.

LEADERSHIP. MAGIC. STORIES. MUSIC. ALL LIVE IN THE AETHER; TO MASTER THEM, YOU MUST MASTER THE 5TH ELEMENT.

Mastering the 5th element is complex. It cannot be taught. It can only be practiced, and your mastery can be better or worse. Fortunately, the learning curve is not steep. Once you start practicing it, you will notice that your self-efficacy increases dramatically. Psychologist Albert Bandura defines self-efficacy[115] as confidence in exerting control over one's motivation, behavior, and social environment. It is a belief in mastery and an ability to recover from failure faster. It is a viewpoint that challenges are something to be mastered rather than threats to avoid.

Originally, I thought believing in the impossible was a magician's "thing." It was easy for me to start working in the imaginary space, as I cognitively ringfenced this around the creation of magic tricks. I would go to work as a leader during the day and only include the imaginary world at night on stage. I don't know when the belief started to bleed into my leadership, as it wasn't a conscious decision. It emerged, and I was not the one noticing it. I have always offered to coach or mentor aspiring leaders if they thought I had anything to offer. That meant I had interactions not just with the people in my own organization but also from other parts of the company. I started to notice a pattern in what they were asking me to teach them.

"How come you always look so confident even on stage in front of a thousand people?"

"How do you manage to innovate and come up with novel viewpoints and ideas consistently?"

"How do you maintain your optimism and belief that we will work this out, whatever this is?"

The questions started to form a pattern, but more importantly, the witty answers from the mentees began to form a pattern as well.

"I know – it's because you're a magician, right?"
They would say with a smile.

Until then, I had pointed at my resume. My resume had a full page of classes and courses next to my university degrees, and not only did I accredit that to my success, but that was also what I taught. I explained how I constantly chased new knowledge, took courses, and went to masterclasses whenever I had the time and/or budget.

I still believe in life-long learning. Knowledge is complex, and you are never done. There is always something you can learn from any situation. Even a conflict can be seen as a learning process. What beliefs and knowledge does the other person have that I don't have for us to have this conflict?

But I started to wonder.

As a magician, I am in full control of the aether. But am I also applying this mentality as a leader? I started to narrate myself as a leader in the discourse of the magician.

"I master the aether – how people perceive me and how I perceive them. Another person cannot make me angry or frustrated unless I allow it to happen. The feeling has to travel through the aether, which is my domain. I am the author of my own story. My narrative lives in the aether, which is my domain."

I began to understand how difficult it can be to hold a leadership position if you allow other people to influence your mood or allow other people to create your narrative.

When facing a leadership challenge, I never flinched for a second, no matter how grand. My employees always saw a leader firmly believing that we could master this challenge, whatever it was. Just because we cannot imagine any possible way to overcome this challenge right now does not mean it is impossible. It just means we must work with an imaginary dimension for a while before attempting to solve it.

It is not self-confidence that the employees see. It is self-efficacy based on my belief that I have mastered the 5th element.

As Henry Ford famously never said: *"Whether you think you can or think you can't, you're right."*

All of a sudden, the Theseus paradox was no longer a paradox. You might remember this thought experiment. Theseus saved the children of Athens from King Minos by escaping to sea, and to commemorate this, the Athenians would keep and maintain the ship, replacing parts as needed. After centuries, every single part of the ship had been replaced, and the Athenians asked themselves: *"Is it still the same ship now that all planks and parts have been replaced?"* When we realize that the ship is not the sum of the parts, but that is it the aether that the parts are carefully encompassing that forms the ship; we understand how it can remain the same across centuries of replenishments.

We have been on a scientific safari, visiting many different fields of science. Mathematics, physics, philosophy, psychology, biology, etc. Yet we end up somewhere between all these sciences. We cannot place the science of leadership and magic into a category. Therefore, using an archaic and outdated metaphor such as the aether might be okay to describe the space where it all happens.

It is in the relationship between people that magic happens and where love, hate, and power struggles exist.

The aether holds big powers. An atom is primarily empty space. If you removed all of the space between the electrons and the nuclei that make up your body, you would take up less than 2 cubic millimetres.

Separating the nothing is what makes atom bombs blow up with devastating power. Separating the aether releases energy. Losing a loved one will likewise release a devastating energy called sorrow, as there is no longer a space between people for love to exist.

The aether holds big potential. Harness the power and become proficient in the aether, and it will be your domain.

THE AETHER IS EVERYTHING, AND IT IS NOTHING AT THE SAME TIME.

And it is where the methodologies we discussed throughout this book live.

The aether is complex, and to understand the aether, you must understand complexity. We spent some quality time together in a bohemian rhapsody of thoughts and ideas, discovering why embracing complexity and discussing outcomes is important instead of outputs. Complexity is the sum of what we can imagine and what is real and the space in between. This is where I live.

I've left forevermore.

And I'm floating in most peculiar way.

And the stars look very different today.

You no doubt noticed along the way that the title of each chapter is also that of a famous song. Perhaps this is why it has resonated with you so deeply – the rhythm of the beat. Maybe you even began to groove a little, your subconscious singing the choruses – anchoring the topics securely.

I'D SAY YOU'RE ABOUT READY TO ENTER THE AETHER

TOO SOON? FEAR NOT; EVERY GREAT SONG HAS A CODA, BUT FIRST, ONE FINAL TRICK FOR YOU.

ENCORE
SWEET DREAMS ARE MADE OF THIS

When I first created this mentalism effect in the late 90s, it was widely acknowledged "in the field". It is a straightforward piece of mind reading. A spectator is thinking of a word, and the mentalist is reading the mind of the spectator, revealing the word.

This particular effect is being praised because it works in multiple languages. I perform in several languages, as do many mentalists who focus on corporate clientele. Having a trick that works equally well in Danish as in English was a treat.

WHO AM I TO DISAGREE?

You ask a spectator from the audience to think of a word. They have a free choice from the following list of words.

"Try not to let me influence your choice of word. I might try to manipulate you subconsciously, but I know you are strong and can withstand my verbal acuity".

In this sentence, you presuppose that you have such a skillset and the ability to manipulate the spectator verbally. This adds not to the effect but to the persona of the skilled mentalist. As with many other mentalism effects, the stronger the persona you build, the stronger the effects are perceived.

HERE ARE THE WORDS:
INTERNET · ORIGINAL · MASSAGE · HOSPITAL
GENERATION · DISPLAY · OPERATION

These are not random words, even though they might seem so. They possess a unique property that allows you to perform a remarkable feat of mind reading. On top of that property, they are also universal words, meaning they exist in several languages.

HERE IS THE PATTERLINE:

"As you are thinking of the word, imagine a white bedsheet hanging between us. It is slightly translucent and is waving softly in the wind. You look down at your hand and notice you are holding a large black spray can. Now slowly, in your mind, write the word that you are merely thinking of on the white sheet".

You are saying this in a soft, soothing voice. The voice pitch is not part of the effect but part of building the mind reader's persona.

"The white bed sheet is waving softly in the wind, and at first, you think it is weird to write with big, black letters on a newly washed white sheet, but as you write the word, it makes a striking image that you can clearly see in your mind."

"Now, make the image of the sheet vivid. Make it big. So big that, if I could read minds, I could clearly see it."

"Yes – you are doing amazing. I can start to see some letters. I can clearly see an A somewhere in the word, correct?"

"Now, the next letter I see is an I, right? And there is an O? No? Oh, it looks like an O. It's actually a D."

You continue to read a few letters before revealing the word "Display".

Let me explain the secret to this trick. It is a secret based on the unique properties of the word list.

It is not the words themselves that possess this property. It is the collection of words that allows you to do the effect.

These words are not just polylingual. Their internal relationship is of a particular nature when it comes to spelling the words. They are carefully selected such that they share letters progressively. This means you only have to get a single letter wrong to determine the exact word they are thinking of. Simulating difficulties in reading the spectator's mind is something you might have done anyway for theatrical effect, this being mind-reading and all. In this case, it is part of the secret to how the trick works.

For all intents and purposes, you are revealing all the correct letters in the word except one. The effect is accomplished by you getting a single "no" unless they are thinking of the word "Generation," in which case you will be correct all the way.

YOU GUESS THE LETTER	IF THEY SAY NO, THE WORD IS
A	INTERNET
I	MASSAGE
O	DISPLAY
N	HOSPITAL
E	ORIGINAL
G	OPERATION

There are several ways to let the "no" go unnoticed, but more often than not, it adds to the effect that mind reading is not easy and straightforward. You can say things like:

"It's not an N, is it"?

If they say "no", you continue with, *"I thought so; it looks more like an H".*

If they say "yes", you continue with *"I thought so, and I also see an E".*

Either way, you will be able to guess the word they are thinking of by magically reading what they write on the white bedsheet and only get one letter wrong. When you get the letter wrong, you are trading that for the information you need. The knowledge of the exact word they are thinking of.

During the coronavirus epidemic in the early 2020s, this trick came back on the map as a mentalism feat that you could do online, as it does not require any other interaction with the spectator than what can be transmitted in an online meeting.

Once you know the word, you may continue to pretend to read letters from the imagined white sheet. You can even add to the effect by saying: "Remember, you do not have to answer out loud. Just think Yes or No when I ask you about a letter". As you are only saying this line after the first "no", you do not need their answer to be verbal, as it is all acting from here on.

Or you can say, *"Remember, you may choose to lie or tell the truth when I ask you if I am reading a letter correctly"* if you want to add Human Lie Detector to your persona.

CODA𝄢

Life is not a problem to be solved but a

REALITY TO BE EXPERIENCED

What an amazing journey I have had. I have lived a life shaped by my passions, and I have never thought about work-life balance because I have been an amateur all my life – doing what I love and loving what I have been doing.

It all began with an unexpected choice of Major when I enrolled in my first university degree.

Computer Science wasn't my first choice when I applied for the university. As a matter of fact, I was leaning toward Classic Studies. It is a field of study that focuses on ancient Greece and Rome's language, literature, history, art, philosophy, and culture. My love for those things clearly shines through in the pages of this book. However, a newfound love made me reconsider. The Commodore 64 had entered my life, and I wasn't done being curious about computers. At the last minute, I added Computer Science as my first choice.

Universities were amongst the first adopters of the Internet. Back then, we didn't have access to the internet from home. The world wide web hadn't been invented yet, and very few people even knew the Internet existed. There was no online shopping and no social networks. Internet was used by scientists, and in that capacity, I got online in 1989. A few years later, the World Wide Web became a thing. This intrigued me, and I started creating web pages early on. I remember being featured in the prestigious Magic Magazine as the first magician with a homepage. I became fascinated with the possibilities of the Internet.

While my Major was all about the use of digital technology in brain science, my curiosity about the possibilities of the internet just kept growing. I had envisioned a different path, that's for sure, and some of my predictions were completely wrong. An old post of mine can still be found online where I criticize the ability to create animated GIFs on a webpage, stating that web pages should only have static content. Otherwise, it would move the viewers' attention from text to images, which I found wrong. Today, more than two-thirds of the internet traffic is dynamic content such as video and audio streaming. I sometimes wonder what the online world would have looked like had I had my way back then.

Little did I know how important the internet would be. No one did. I was simply chasing a rabbit that I found intriguing.

I have lived a wonderful life chasing interesting magic rabbits. When the iconic record label His Master's Voice (you know – the one with a dog looking into an old fashioned turntable record player) turned 100 years old, I was asked to be the face of the 100-year campaign, doing various forms of magic in TV commercials. There I was, a shy technology leader with magic as a hobby, airing on all TV channels.

When internet service providers and online companies began to show up in the mid-90s, I already had a lot of experience in the field and quickly became involved with building internet solutions. Specifically, I was part of the team building the first e-commerce sites. That was before online credit card payments, so the process of paying was a whole area of its own, which included installing a digital wallet on your computer. All this is to say that by the time the .com and e-commerce bubble was roaring, I already had several years of e-commerce experience and could tell the wheat from the chaff.

Combining that with the tells from deception detection I had learned as a mentalist meant I renewed my interest in using this skill professionally. I noticed that the same people who obviously believed in their idea at the first investment rounds now clearly showed signs of disbelief when they were talking about the bright future for their online product on the news. At that time, I was teaching e-commerce as a side gig. I still have the slides from back then. They were not PowerPoint but physical transparent pieces of plastic placed on an overhead projector. I saw the same disbelief in my student's eyes when I showed a graph projecting how much of our shopping we would be doing online in the future.

Remember, this is the late 90s, so the future I was talking about is already our past. My statements made enough waves to give me a narrative of someone who understands what the internet is about. When another company wanted to build an online department, my narrative probably brought me to an unexpected career change. On the first day of the new millennium, I changed jobs for the first time. Little did I know that I would only do that once more in my lifetime.

"Soon, applications will be consumed on phones, not computers", I remember imagining. This was seven years before the iPhone saw the day of light. It couldn't have been easy being my leader back then, as the claims I made were, at the time, somewhat out there. Yet I was still given the space to explore the idea of using a mobile phone to do more than make calls. I would like to express my gratitude to Stibo, the company I worked for at the time, for providing the space for this to evolve.

My first "mobile app" was an email client I made for personal use. I wanted to read email even when I was away from my computer, and

I realized I always had a device with a display on me. I had a Linux server running, fetching my email, and based on some heuristics, it would send me a text message with the gist of the mail. Who it was from, and the first couple of lines, stripping any attachments. I could reply back by using a simple markup language. It wasn't so much a mobile app as it was a mobile service, but that came soon after.

Around the same time as I started my job, mobile devices got a new capability called WAP (Wireless Application Protocol), and my Nokia 6110 could run WAP. Think of WAP as very basic HTML pages on a very limited display. What possibilities were hidden behind this door?

My first professional mobile app was for a customer with technicians driving around the country to fix equipment. GPS wasn't widely available then, so the technicians relied on paper maps for navigation. My app was a turn-by-turn WAP navigation system they could use on their phones. The technicians would enter their current location and destination into a form on the app, giving them text-based directions just like what we're used to with GPS today - for example, "drive 400 meters then turn left on Orange Street".

While this may be a commodity today, it was quite novel around the turn of the millennium to use a phone as a handheld device for navigation and to use digital guidance instead of paper maps. This is a wonderful part of my unexpected journey because not only was it not planned, no one could have predicted it.

Working on products no one could imagine on technology that had just emerged was amazing and impossible to expect.

I am not more creative, nor do I have more foresight than anyone else. Being a frontrunner on the internet, on e-commerce, and on mobile apps was not due to me being more intelligent than the rest; it was due to curiosity and the desire to chase magic rabbits as they appeared. It was the desire to use my imagination.

When I studied mathematics, no one questioned the addition of imaginary numbers. It was clear that the extra dimension would help mathematics in many ways. Moving a problem into the complex space to take advantage of the extra dimension was obviously helpful. This may have helped condition my approach to accept that not only math can be improved by the imaginary. A beautiful little gem from math is that sometimes, real=imagination.

An example of this, to all you mathematicians out there, with a nod to Euler[5]: $i^i = e^{-\frac{\pi}{2}}$. The beauty of this formula is that the left-hand side is purely imaginary, and the right-hand side is all real numbers. This proves that the path from imagination to reality is possible without "taking a leap" across some magical boundary. It's a continuous journey. If you are not into math, this equation will make little sense, but please indulge me in catering to a branch of science that can be quite inspirational, albeit a bit nerdy sometimes.

We talked about the camel principle before. Here is an example where something is added, solving a problem, only to be taken away again. Fibonacci numbers: 1,1,2,3,5,8... each number is the sum of the two preceding numbers. We see this sequence in many places in nature: The number of petals in a lily flower or seed heads in a sunflower, tree branches, and the shape of seashells. All very natural shapes (as they are found in nature), yet they all follow the Fibonacci sequence. The strange thing is that the formula for Fibonacci numbers[6] includes irrational numbers ($\sqrt{5}$ and the golden ratio φ, just in case you're interested). The irrational part disappears at some point during the process, but it is needed to get to the rational and natural solution. We add a camel and take it back.

---

[5]Because $i^i = e^{\ln(i^i)} = e^{i\ln(i)} = e^{i\frac{i\pi}{2}} = e^{-\frac{\pi}{2}}$ combined with Euler's formula

[6]Known as Binet's formula

This was a step towards understanding that everything is possible. When a magician devises new tricks and effects, it happens in the imagination where "possible" is not a limitation. When the trick is done, ready to perform for an audience, the preferred reaction from the spectators is: "That's impossible!" or "That's wonderful!" Creating magic is not unlike developing new products or developing people. It works wonderfully when everything is possible. The burden of reality is gone, and the cognitive load of only thinking about possibilities is lifted. This frees the mind to be even more creative and find even better solutions. The ability to behave in this way comes from the knowledge of illusion questions. The secret methods that magicians and leaders use to transcend something from imagination to reality. By asking illusion questions, ideas transcend into real hypotheses, ready for a reality check.

MODERN LEADERSHIP IS ABOUT CREATING THE SPACE FOR THE AGENCY TO EVOLVE AND FOR EMERGENCE TO HAPPEN.

The population of ideas is plenty, and we need to train the curiosity muscle to catch them. Good ideas emerge in the imaginary space all the time, and with the proper agency, we are more inclined to discover them. I owe a big thanks to my leaders at that time, enabling me to work on emerging technologies and ideas and breaking early ground on some things that would greatly impact our daily lives.

My first book described modern leadership – specifically in a digital world. I wrote the book "Wonderful Digital Leadership", and quite unexpectedly, this was picked up as curriculum for a triple crown accredited MBA. My lectures were conducted as interviews between the professors and me, discussing various aspects of leadership in a digital world.

While some may say that these unexpected opportunities were more luck or serendipity than due to my consciousness of curiosity, I will say that even serendipity can be increased. There's a fine paper called *"Towards a Theory of Serendipity: A Systematic Review and Conceptualization*[116]*"*. In this paper, the principles of serendipity are laid out scientifically.

Either way you look at it, I feel blessed.

Being among the first on the internet, floating around, imagining what this could become.

Doing mobile apps back when it was unthinkable that we would spend hours a day staring at our phones, and even owning a mobile phone was a rarity.

All this because I was taking the mentality and toolbox of a magician with me to work.

I stayed at the same place for a decade. Then, I switched jobs for the last time. After only working in the technology industry, my next endeavor was unexpected – a toy company.

When I drove to work on the first day of the new year, it was not the 10-minute drive I was used to. I was driving to the LEGO Group headquarters in Billund, Denmark.

I wanted to work on something that made sense and not just maximize shareholder value. After my last company was acquired by a competitor, I felt it was all about earning money and little about having a mission. I had heard the owner of the LEGO Group saying, that their mission was to bring play to children of the world, which inspired me.

Now, having worked here for more than a decade, I have never heard the owner talk about profit even once. The only time the owner talks about money is in relation to altruism and donating to various charities. I wanted to work there, and as fate wanted it, a headhunter called me about an exciting job in the toy industry. I was carrying a narrative of an innovative thought leader, which helped me land an excellent position at the LEGO Group. I did not see myself as a thought leader, and I probably wasn't one either. But as the expectations towards me grew, so did my efficacy and belief that I could live up to the narrative of being a thought leader. This was the year I started working on my second Master's, writing a thesis on the power of narratives. Outside of my research, I began to understand how complexity theory could create better leaders, and I created the ideas of agency and dynamic focus in complexity.

Complexity is something that needs to be embraced. Traditionally, we have the urge to simplify. Break a problem down. Eat the elephant bit by bit. But the reductive tendency in complexity causes more harm than good[117].

Bringing the ideas of agency and dynamic focus into the complex world of leadership was a major driver in my work on the global leadership model for the LEGO Group. However, I initially had mixed feelings when I saw the Leadership Playground in action. It's hard to explain what they were, but it reminded me of an episode in the early 90s. I was studying at the university, and like all hard-working students, I went out on Friday nights. I remember thinking that it was strange that no clubs had decent music. I was into rock and blues and had been for many years, but all they played was pop and disco. Then Gary Moore released his hit album "Still got the Blues", with guest contributions from blues icons Albert King, Albert Collins, and George Harrison.

Now, the clubs would finally play blues, and you would meet people saying, "Oh, I'm really into blues – I like Gary Moore". So, on the one hand, I got what I wanted – more music to my taste. On the other hand, none of these new joiners to the genre had walked the path I had walked, and it felt like their interest was not as genuine.

In the beginning, I had the same experience when talking about leadership with colleagues at The LEGO Group. It is a bit embarrassing to admit in writing, but I initially felt like they had gotten the baby without going through labor. Fortunately, this feeling was only in passing because I had a completely different view after a few months. The Leadership Playground gave these leaders a shared language, not capabilities. They were already seasoned and capable leaders, and there was no reason to say they hadn't "earned the stripes". Now, when discussing leadership, we shared the language and discourse, and it was easier for everybody to share their knowledge and experience.

I became more aware of leading from purpose and to embrace the magician as part of the leader. At one point, we hired Core Leadership Institute to help each of us identify and lead from purpose.[118] My official "LEGO" purpose is: *"The magician bringing imagination into reality"*. This purpose shaped my leadership and my approach to innovation and creativity. As I lived my purpose, the borderline between the magician and the Vice President blurred. I began to encourage that innovation workshops should start by disavowing the limitations of reality, and I found that, as a leader, my words were creating just as big an impact as my actions.

I became more interested in how the arena of human interaction is language. Not just when we are creating or discussing leadership models but in general.

Language is not a neutral tool for communication but rather an integral part of the way we perceive and interact with the world. The Chilean biologist and philosopher Humberto Maturana believed that language shapes our understanding of reality and influences the way we think and behave. In this sense, "languaging[119]" is a fundamental aspect of human cognition and social interaction. He defines the odd word "languaging" as the process by which individuals use language to create and communicate meaning. It is not just a matter of using words to convey information but rather a way of constructing and shaping our reality through the use of language.

This led me down a veritable rabbit hole of social constructionism. Social constructionism is a sociological and anthropological perspective focusing on how social phenomena are constructed through human interaction and communication. It suggests that the reality we experience is not fixed or objective but rather is shaped and influenced by the social, cultural, and historical contexts in which we live. According to social constructionism, people's beliefs, values, and behaviors are not simply the result of individual psychology or biology but are shaped and influenced by the social groups and institutions to which they belong. This means that what we consider reality is not necessarily objective or universal but is constructed through our interactions with others and the cultural frameworks we operate within. A critical aspect of social constructionism is the idea that knowledge and meaning are not simply discovered or transmitted but are actively constructed through social interactions and communication. This indicates that the ways we understand and make sense of the world are not simply based on objective facts but are shaped by the social and cultural contexts in which we live.

The study of social constructionism brought me to the science of personal and organizational narratives. I took my second Master's while working at the LEGO Group, and I am grateful to work for a company that invested the time and money into further educating me. I used much of what I learned in my day job, so I feel the investment was worth it, and I believe the feeling is mutual. I spent the better part of a decade doing action learning studies, verifying what we discussed in the chapter about you versus your narrative. I was particularly interested in how narratives drive action more than the other way around. During that period, many people approached me for coaching, and I learned a lot from working with different people with different challenges and narratives.

Learning has always been central. I always felt a bit sad when graduating and finishing courses. There is so much out there to learn. Before we created the global leadership model, I had created a local model for my own business unit at the LEGO Group. While they do look similar, they differ in a key area: Learning. In my local leadership model, I wanted to create the space for the employees to learn in order to achieve the five bullet points we discussed in the chapter on the power of learning.

Ethical behavior is essential for preserving social cohesion and maintaining harmonious relationships within society. It is not a matter of choice but rather a necessary aspect of human nature and how we interact with others[120]. Ethics was important as I moved the science of influence from the realm of entertainment into my professional work. I found that most of the techniques I used as a mentalist to control the behavior of others were directly transferable. When doing mind-control as entertainment, the ethical part is done by framing this as entertainment and clearly stating what is about to happen or explaining what happened afterward. When it comes to the narrative aspects, it was relatively easy to keep the people I was coaching honest because, as it turned out, creating a false narrative, or even lying about things, is difficult and short-lived.

But when it comes to influencing, it was a different beast. Right at the time I started working professionally with moving influence techniques from entertainment into organizational theory, the world around me also used some of the same words but in different contexts. It was at the beginning of social media "influencers" and the birth of "nudging". I was averse to these new players in the arena for various reasons.

People got to be influencers on social media by doing things that elicited emotions and actions from the viewers. That quickly meant they did stupid things or said controversial things to get likes and rise on the influencer scale. Nudging was another new word that we had to get used to[121]. The concept of nudging as a tool for shaping behavior can be traced back to the work of psychologists and behavioral economists in the mid-20th century, who studied how small changes in the context or framing of a decision could influence people's choices.

What bothered me with nudging and the whole idea of influencing people's choices was that it assumed that the person doing the nudging knew best. But remember when we were all asked to consider using asbestos to insulate our houses because of the unique properties of asbestos being durable, fireproof, and insulating? Today, we know better. Whom should we trust to influence the behavior of others, and who watches the watchmen? And because nudging is what it is – a nudge – it is not always apparent to people when they are being nudged, and then it becomes manipulation.

With that, I had some concerns writing about the language of mentalists. The *"language within the language"* can be used to accomplish the exact things that I was repelled by. Reading scholars debating similar considerations in different arenas convinced me that I could describe this ethically. I was particularly inspired by the cognitive psychologist and memory researcher Elizabeth Loftus who created much transparency on how eyewitnesses can be manipulated and false memories implanted during what seemed like a standard courtroom procedure[122]. This transparency into the material and methods helped create awareness and reduce unethical behavior.

The more people learn from this, the better.

Still, the connection to the aether and the "white space" between meanings was apparent. I never bought into any of the analogies that were put forth to represent an organization. An organization is not a living organism; it is not a machine, nor is it anything else but a word we use for our internal sensemaking. The organization is not even the people, it is the relationship between them and the stories told among them.

My day job at the LEGO Group is creating digital solutions that delight consumers. My work on shaping the way we do leadership is driven by passion, not as a "side gig" but as an integral part of my work. My department might be digital, and I probably got to the level I am because of my digital merits as a front-runner on online and mobile solutions. However, my pride and legacy are my work with and for people, not technology.

As I am reaching the end of my personal journey, my reasons for writing this book are to shape my narrative and legacy. I have no desire to be remembered as a technological front-runner. I do not build software. I build people. I am a leader, a magician, a father, a husband and a friend. My passion is people. My contribution is a leadership philosophy that hopefully will help other humans embark on unexpected leadership journeys.

As I write the final words, I can't help but feel a sense of gratitude for the remarkable life I've led. As a magician and leader, I've had the honor of sharing my passion with the world, leaving a trail of wonder and inspiration in my wake. Now, as I prepare to embark on the greatest adventure of all, I hope that the legacy I leave behind will continue to inspire, uplift, and bring joy to those who follow in my footsteps. And so, with a heart full of love and gratitude, I say my final farewell to you, dear reader, and may the magic live on in your hearts forever.

REFERENCES

[1] Hogan, Kevin (2006). Covert Hypnosis: An operators manual. Network 3000 publishing.

[2] Arce, R., Selaya, A., Sanmarco, J., & Fariña, F. (2023). Implanting rich autobiographical false memories: Meta–analysis for forensic practice and judicial judgment making. International Journal of Clinical and Health Psychology, 23

[3] Dalla Barba, G., & La Corte, V. (2013). Confabulation. In S. K. Whitbourne (Ed.), The encyclopedia of clinical psychology (Vol. 1-5). Wiley-Blackwell.

[4] Slepian, M. L., Chun, J. S., & Mason, M. F. (2017). The experience of secrecy. Journal of Personality and Social Psychology, 113(1), 1-33.

[5] Aksnes, Dag. Langeldt, Liv. Wouters, Paul (2019). "Citations, Citation Indicators, and Research Quality: An Overview of Basic Concepts and Theories". SAGE open, January-march 2019

[6] Weisberg, D. S., Landrum, A. R., Hamilton, J., & Weisberg, M. (2021). "Knowledge about the nature of science increases public acceptance of science regardless of identity factors". Public Understanding of Science, 30(2), 120–138.

[7] Pablo Villalobos et al. (2022), "Will we run out of ML data? Evidence from projecting dataset size trends". Published online at epochai.org. Retrieved from: 'https://epochai.org/blog/will-we-run-out-of-ml-data-evidence-from-projecting-dataset

[8] Benedek, M., Karstendiek, M., Ceh, S. M., Grabner, R. H., Krammer, G., Lebuda, I., Silvia, P. J., Cotter, K. N., Li, Y., Hu, W., Martskvishvili, K., & Kaufman, J. C. (2021). Creativity myths: Prevalence and correlates of misconceptions on creativity. Personality and Individual Differences, 182, 111068. ISSN 0191-8869.

[9] Fink, T.M.A., Reeves, M., Palma, R. et al. Serendipity and strategy in rapid innovation. Nat Commun 8, 2002 (2017).

[10] De Shazer, S., & Berg, I. K. (1984). The miracle question. Family Process, 23(3), 371-385

[11] Heifetz, R. A., & Linsky, M. (2002). Leadership on the line: Staying alive through the dangers of leading. Boston: Harvard Business Review Press.

[12] De Shazer, S., & Berg, I. K. (1988). Keys to solution in brief therapy. New York: Norton.

[13] Goldratt, E. M. (1984). The Goal: A Process of Ongoing Improvement. North River Press.

[14] Razzouk, R., & Shute, V. (2012). What is design thinking and why is it important? Review of Educational Research, 82, 330-348

[15] Groeger, L., & Schweitzer, J. (2014). Transformational leadership, design thinking, and the innovative organization.

[16] Senge, P. M. (2006). The fifth discipline: The art and practice of the learning organization. New York: Doubleday.

[17] Argyris, C., & Schön, D. (1982). Organization learning: A theory of action perspective. Reading, MA: Addison-Wesley.

[18] Hero (1899). "Pneumatika, Book II, Chapter XI". Herons von Alexandria Druckwerke und Automatentheater (in Greek and German). Wilhelm Schmidt (translator). Leipzig: B.G. Teubner

[19] Netz, R., & Noel, W. (2004). Heron of Alexandria: Mechanics and optics. Cambridge University Press.

[20] Cottingham, John (1996). René Descartes: Meditations on First Philosophy with Selections from the Objections and Replies. Cambridge: Cambridge University Press.

[21] Pacioli, Luca (1494). Summa de arithmetica, geometria, proportioni et proportionalita. Paganini.

[22] Arnaldo Camuffo, Alessandro Cordova, Alfonso Gambardella, Chiara Spina (2019) A Scientific Approach to Entrepreneurial Decision Making: Evidence from a Randomized Control Trial. Management Science 66(2):564-586.

[23] Taylor, F. W. (1911). The principles of scientific management. Harper and Brothers.

[24] Frank, D., Kafkas, A., & Montaldi, D. (2022). Experiencing Surprise: The Temporal Dynamics of Its Impact on Memory. Journal of Neuroscience, 42(33)

[25] Gras, David & Conger, Michael & Jenkins, Anna & Gras, Michael. (2019). Wicked problems, reductive tendency, and the formation of (non-)opportunity beliefs. Journal of Business Venturing.

[26] Rittel, H. W. J., & Webber, M. M. (1973). Dilemmas in a general theory of planning. Policy Sciences, 4(2), 155-169.

[27] Andersen, Christian Vandsø (2022). "Wonderful Digital Leadership". Plazeebo Publishing.

[28] The Cobra Effect: "Good Intentions, Perverse Outcomes". Psychology Today. Retrieved 29 March 2021.

[29] Christopher Newfield, Anna Alexandrova, Stephen John (2022) University of Chicago Press, Social Science

[30] Denrell Jerker, Liu Chengwei (2012) "Top performers are not the most impressive when extreme performance indicates unreliability". Proceedings of the National Academy of Sciences vol 109.

[31] Collins, Jim. (2001). Good to Great. London, England: Random House Business Books.

[32] Lifchits, George et al (2021). Judgment and Decision Making, Vol. 16, No. 6, November 2021, pp. 1439–1463

[33] Characterization and engineering of aplastic-degrading aromatic polyesterase (2018). Austin, Harry P. et al. Proceedings of the National Academy of Sciences Volume 115, Issue 19

[34] Lydia Paine Hagtvedt, Karyn Dossinger, Spencer H. Harrison, Li Huang (2019). Curiosity made the cat more creative: Specific curiosity as a driver of creativity, Organizational Behavior and Human Decision Processes, Volume 150

[35] Simons DJ, Chabris CF. (1999) Gorillas in our midst: sustained inattentional blindness for dynamic events. Perception. 1999;28(9):1059–1074.

[36] Drew T, Võ ML, Wolfe JM. (2013) The invisible gorilla strikes again: sustained inattentional blindness in expert observers. Psychol Sci. 2013 Sep;24(9):1848-53.

[37] Zeiträg, C., Jensen, T. R., & Osvath, M. (2022). Gaze following: A socio-cognitive skill rooted in deep time. Frontiers in Psychology, 13.

[38] Abi-Esber, Nicole, Alison Wood Brooks, and Ethan Burris. "Feeling Seen: Leader Eye Gaze Promotes Psychological Safety, Participation, and Voice." Harvard Business School Working Paper, No. 22-048, January 2022

[39] Hoelsmann, J. Manso, G. (2022). "The Streetlight Effect in Data-Driven Exploration." UC Berkeley.

[40] Revonsuo, A.; Newman, J. (Jun 1999). "Binding and consciousness". Conscious Cogn

[41] Feldman JA. (2006) From molecule to metaphor: a neural theory of language. Cambridge: MIT Press;

[42] Yu, Xinchi, and Ellen Lau. (2022). "The Binding Problem 2.0: Beyond Perceptual Features." PsyArXiv. October 31

[43] Di Lollo, Vincent. (2012). The feature-binding problem is an ill-posed problem. Trends in cognitive sciences. 16.

[44] O'Connor, Timothy, "Emergent Properties", The Stanford Encyclopedia of Philosophy (Winter 2021 Edition), Edward N. Zalta (ed.)

[45] Dora, J., van Hooff, M., Geurts, S., Kompier, M., & Bijleveld, E. (2021). Fatigue, boredom and objectively measured smartphone use at work. Royal Society Open Science, 8(7), 201915

[46] Andreasen, N. C. (2005). The creating brain: The neuroscience of genius. Dana Press.

[47] Taleb, Nassim Nicholas (2010) [2007]. The Black Swan: The Impact of the Highly Improbable (2nd ed.). London: Penguin

[48] D. Sornette, Dragon-Kings, Black Swans and the Prediction of Crises, International Journal of Terraspace Science and Engineering 1(3), 1–17 (2009)

[49] Shaw, George; Nodder, Frederick Polydore (1799). "The Duck-Billed Platypus, Platypus anatinus". The Naturalist's Miscellany.

[50] Maes, M., Leunis, J. C., Geffard, M., & Berk, M. (2012). Evidence for the existence of Myalgic Encephalomyelitis/Chronic Fatigue Syndrome (ME/CFS) with and without abdominal discomfort (irritable bowel) syndrome. Neuroendocrinology Letters, 33(2), 188-197.

[51] Wittgenstein, Ludwig (1922). Tractatus Logico-Philosophicus. W. Ostwald Annalen der Naturphilosophie

[52] Piaget, Jean (1932). The Moral Judgment of the Child. Free press.

[53] Lepper, M. R., Greene, D., & Nisbett, R. E. (1973). Undermining children's intrinsic interest with extrinsic reward: A test of the "overjustification" hypothesis. Journal of Personality and Social Psychology, 28(1),

54 Pink, D. H. (2011). Drive: The Surprising Truth About What Motivates Us. Penguin.

55 Collings VB. Human taste response as a function of location of stimulation on the tongue and soft palate. Percept Psychophys . 1974;16:169-174.

56 Knoll, A. R., Otani, H., Skeel, R. L., & Van Horn, K. R. (2017). Learning style, judgements of learning, and learning of verbal and visual information. British Journal of Psychology, 108(3), 544-563.

57 An, D., & Carr, M. (2017). Learning styles theory fails to explain learning and achievement: Recommendations for alternative approaches. Personality and Individual Differences, 116, 410-416.

58 Elsaadawy, N., & Carlson, E. N. (2022). Do you make a better or worse impression than you think? Journal of Personality and Social Psychology, 123(6), 1407–1420

59 Graca da Silva S, Tehrani JJ. 2016 Comparative phylogenetic analyses uncover the ancient roots of Indo-European folktales. R.soc.open sci. 3: 150645.

60 Barbieri et al (2022). "A global analysis of matches and mismatches between human genetic and linguistic histories." Proceedings of the National Academy of Sciences.

61 Fritz Breithaupt, Binyan Li & John K. Kruschke (2022) Serial reproduction of narratives preserves emotional appraisals, Cognition and Emotion, 36:4, 581-601

62 Scientists Trace Society's Myths to Primordial Origins" in Scientific American 315, 6, 62-69 (December 2016)

63 Jung, C. G. (1959). The archetypes and the collective unconscious (R. F. C. Hull, Trans.). Princeton University Press.

64 Mead, George Herbert (1967). Mind, Self, and Society from the Standpoint of a Social Behaviorist. Chicago: The University of Chicago Press.

65 Gergen, Kenneth (1985) The Social Construction of the Person. New York: Springer-Verlag,

66 Gergen, Kenneth (1999) An Invitation to Social Construction. London: Sage

67 Gergen, Kenneth (1992). The Saturated Self, Dilemmas of Identity in Contemporary Life. New York: Basic Books

[68] Rosenthal and Jacobson (1968). Pygmalion in the classroom

[69] Jussim, L., & Harber, K. D. (2005). Teacher Expectations and Self-Fulfilling Prophecies: Knowns and Unknowns, Resolved and Unresolved Controversies. Personality and Social Psychology Review, 9(2), 131–155.

[70] Franz, D.J., Richter, T., Lenhard, W. et al. The Influence of Diagnostic Labels on the Evaluation of Students: a Multilevel Meta-Analysis. Educ Psychol Rev 35, 17 (2023). https://doi.org/10.1007/s10648-023-09716-6

[71] Giddens, Anthony (1991) Modernity and Self-Identity. Self and Society in the Late Modern Age. Cambridge Press

[72] Shotter, John. (1993) Conversational Realities: Constructing Life Through Language. Sage Publications

[73] Ibañez, J. P. (2013). Body mentalism. Bazar de Magia.

[74] Pailhes, Alice; Rensink, Ronald A. and Kuhn, Gustav. 2020. A psychologically based taxonomy of Magicians' forcing Techniques: How magicians influence our choices, and how to use this to study psychological mechanisms. Consciousness and Cognition, 86, 103038. ISSN 1053-8100 [Article]

[75] Torres, N (2014). "Most people don't want to be managers". Harward Business Review. September 18 2014

[76] Anderson, Cameron & Sharps, Daron & Soto, Christopher & John, Oliver. (2020). People with disagreeable personalities (selfish, combative, and manipulative) do not have an advantage in pursuing power at work. Proceedings of the National Academy of Sciences.

[77] van der Linden, S. (2023). Foolproof: Why misinformation infects our minds and how to build immunity. New York: Random House

[78] Dante R. Chialvo , "How we hear what is not there: A neural mechanism for the missing fundamental illusion", Chaos 13, 1226-1230 (2003)

[79] Rohde M, Di Luca M, Ernst MO. The Rubber Hand Illusion: feeling of ownership and proprioceptive drift do not go hand in hand. PLoS One. 2011;6(6):e21659

[80] Troxler, D. (I. P. V.) (1804). Himly, K.; Schmidt, J.A. (eds.). "Über das Verschwinden gegebener Gegenstände innerhalb unseres Gesichtskreises" Ophthalmologische Bibliothek (in German). 2 (2):

[81] Hargadon, Andrew and Douglas Yellowless (2001). "When innovations meet institutions: Edison and the design of the electric light." Cornvell University.

[82] Freeberg, E. (2013). The age of Edison: Electric light and the invention of modern America. New York: Penguin Press

[83] Xu, M., & Wegener, D. T. (2023). Persuasive Benefits of Self-Generated Arguments: Moderation and Mechanism. Social Psychological and Personality Science, 0(0)

[84] Bandler, R., & Grinder, J. (1975). The structure of magic II: A book about communication and change. Palo Alto, CA: Science and Behavior Books.

[85] Loftus, Elizabeth; Ketcham, Katherine (1991). Witness for the Defense: The Accused, the Eyewitness, and the Expert Who Puts Memory On Trial. New York: St. Martin's Press

[86] Prasad, Deepasri, and Wilma A. Bainbridge. "The Visual Mandela Effect as Evidence for Shared and Specific False Memories Across People." PsyArXiv, 25 May 2021

[87] Siew, C. S. Q., Engelthaler, T., & Hills, T. T. (2022). Nymph piss and gravy orgies: Local and global contrast effects in relational humor. Journal of Experimental Psychology: Learning, Memory, and Cognition, 48(7), 1047–1063.

[88] Kant, I. (1914). Kant's Critique of Judgement (revised)(JH Bernard, Trans.). London, UK: Macmillan.(Original work published in German 1790).

[89] Jakubowski, K., & Ghosh, A. (2021). Music-evoked autobiographical memories in everyday life. Psychology of Music, 49(3), 649–666.

[90] Fusaroli, R , Raczaszek-Leonardi, J., & Tylen, K. (2016). The musical nature of speech: Investigating the activation and imitation of speech melody. Neuroscience & Biobehavioral Reviews, 68, 612-621.

[91] Peretz, I., & Zatorre, R. J. (2005). Brain organization for music processing. Annual Review of Psychology, 56, 89-114.

[92] Coupé, Christophe et al (2019) Different languages, similar encoding efficiency: Comparable information rates across the human communicative niche.Science Advances

[93] Van Zant, A. B., & Berger, J. (2019, June 13). How the Voice Persuades. Journal of Personality and Social Psychology. Advance online publication

[94] Trager, G. L. (1958). Paralanguage: A first approximation. Studies in Linguistics, 13, 1–12.

[95] John Antonakis, Giovanna d'Adda, Roberto A. Weber, Christian Zehnder (2022) "Just Words? Just Speeches?" On the Economic Value of Charismatic Leadership. Management Science 68(9):6355-6381.

[96] Buckley, A. (1947). Card control: A post graduate course on practical methods. Self published.

[97] Kaltsas, A. C., Zampelas, A., & Papadopoulos, A. K. (2021). The gut-brain axis: How microbiota and diet influence the brain. Advances in Nutrition, 12(1), 49-60.

[98] Oeberst, A., & Imhoff, R. (2023). Toward Parsimony in Bias Research: A Proposed Common Framework of Belief-Consistent Information Processing for a Set of Biases. Perspectives on Psychological Science, 0(0).

[99] Coles, N.A., March, D.S., Marmolejo-Ramos, F. et al. A multi-lab test of the facial feedback hypothesis by the Many Smiles Collaboration. Nat Hum Behav (2022).

[100] James, W. (1890). The Principles of Psychology. Henry Holt and Company.

[101] Damasio, A. R. (1994). Descartes' error: Emotion, reason, and the human brain. New York: Putnam.

[102] Clark, A. (1997). Being there: Putting brain, body, and world together again. Cambridge, MA: MIT Press.

[103] Murray, D. R., Haselton, M. G., Fales, M., & Cole, S. W. (2019). Falling in love is associated with immune system gene regulation. Psychoneuroendocrinology, 100, 120-126

[104] Bandler, R., & Grinder, J. (1975). The Structure of Magic, Vol. I. Science and Behavior Books.

[105] Descartes, R. (1641). Meditations on First Philosophy. In J. Cottingham, R. Stoothoff, D. Murdoch, & A. Kenny (Eds.), The Philosophical Writings of Descartes (Vol. 2, pp. 12-53). Cambridge University Press

[106] Premack, D. (1985). The Infant's Theory of Self-Propelled Objects. In D. R. Rogers & J. A. Sloboda (Eds.), The Acquisition of Symbolic Skills (pp. 1-16). Plenum Press.

[107] Leslie, A. M. (1987). Pretense and representation: The origins of "theory of mind." Psychological Review, 94(4), 412-426.

[108] Baron-Cohen, S., Jolliffe, T., Mortimore, C., & Robertson, M. (1997). Another advanced test of theory of mind: Evidence from very high functioning adults with autism or Asperger syndrome. Journal of Child Psychology and Psychiatry, 38(7), 813-822.

[109] Forer, B. R. (1948). The fallacy of personal validation: A classroom demonstration of gullibility. Journal of Abnormal and Social Psychology, 43(3), 118-121.

[110] Sagarin, B. J., & Skowronski, J. J. (1998). The Forer effect revisited: Varying the length of personalized feedback. Journal of Social Psychology, 138(3), 267-272.

[111] Siegel, D. J., & Bryson, T. P. (2011). The whole-brain child: 12 revolutionary strategies to nurture your child's developing mind. New York: Delacorte Press.

[112] Oktar, K., & Lombrozo, T. (2022). Deciding to be authentic: Intuition is favored over deliberation when authenticity matters. Cognition, 223, 105021.

[113] Landsberger, H. A. (1958). Hawthorne Revisited. Ithaca.

[114] Jay A. Olson, Mariève Cyr, Despina Z. Artenie, Thomas Strandberg, Lars Hall, Matthew L. Tompkins, Amir Raz, Petter Johansson (2023). "Emulating future neurotechnology using magic" Consciousness and Cognition,Volume 107

[115] Bandura, A (1977) "Self-efficacy: Toward a Unifying Theory of Behavioral Change". Psychological Review. 84 (2): 191–215.

[116] Busch, C. (2022), Towards a Theory of Serendipity: A Systematic Review and Conceptualization. J. Manage. Stud.

[117] Gras, David et. al (2019) "Wicked problems, reductive tendency, and the formation of (non-)opportunity beliefs". Journal of Business Venturing. Sept. 2019

[118] Craig, Nick. Snook, Scott. (2014). "From Purpose to Impact". Harvard Business Review May 2014

[119] Maturana, H., & Varela, F. (1987). The tree of knowledge: The biological roots of human understanding. Boston: Shambhala.

[120] Maturana, H. (1998). The origin of humanness in the biology of love. Inverness, CA: Edgepress

[121] Thaler, R., & Sunstein, C. (2008). Nudge: Improving Decisions About Health, Wealth, and Happiness. New Haven, CT: Yale University Press.

[122] Loftus, E. (2003). The manipulative use of language. In S. O. Lilienfeld, I. D. D. MacCrae, & J Ruscio (Eds.), Psychological science in the public interest (Vol. 4, pp. 27-44). Washington, DC: American Psychological Association.

Printed in Poland
by Amazon Fulfillment
Poland Sp. z o.o., Wrocław

31889047R00161